D1441889

OUR PROMISED LAND

OUR PROMISED LAND

Faith and Militant Zionism in Israeli Settlements

Charles Selengut

ROWMAN & LITTLEFIELD
Lanham • Boulder • New York • London

Published by Rowman & Littlefield
A wholly owned subsidiary of
The Rowman & Littlefield Publishing Group, Inc.
4501 Forbes Boulevard, Suite 200, Lanham, Maryland 20706
www.rowman.com

Unit A, Whitacre Mews, 26-34 Stannary Street, London SE11 4AB,
United Kingdom

British Library Cataloguing in Publication Information Available

Library of Congress Cataloging-in-Publication Data
Selengut, Charles, author.
Our promised land : faith and militant Zionism in Israeli settlements / Charles
Selengut.
pages cm
Includes bibliographical references and index.
ISBN 978-1-4422-1685-3 (cloth : alk. paper) — ISBN 978-1-4422-1687-7
(electronic : alk. paper)
1. Land settlement—West Bank—History—21st century. 2. Land settlement—Government policy—Israel. 3. Jews—West Bank—Politics and government—21st century. 4. Israelis—West Bank—Politics and government—21st
century. 5. West Bank—Politics and government—21st century. 6. West
Bank—Ethnic relations. 7. Arab-Israeli conflict—Influence. I. Title. II. Title:
Faith and militant Zionism in Israeli settlements.
HD850.5.Z63.S46 2015
333.3'156953089924—dc23
2015008613

Printed in the United States of America

CONTENTS

ACKNOWLEDGMENTS

Professor Peter Berger, my teacher at the graduate faculty of New School University, taught that social reality is constructed and maintained through ongoing human conversation, in the give and take of dialogue and human interaction. Talking with another, whether in agreement or disagreement, in a personal, face-to-face interaction, is among the most profound and uniquely human experiences. Books, as social productions, have their genesis in conversation and interaction. *Our Promised Land* is the result of many conversations, dialogues, and even heated disagreements with friends, colleagues, and students, and I want to thank them and express my appreciation and gratitude. The views and positions in this book are, however, mine alone, and none of these scholars are necessarily in agreement with the views and perspective taken in this work.

I want to thank my colleague, Professor Jill Schennum, with whom I discussed many issues concerning aspects of religion and state in contemporary society. Professor Schennum read the manuscript as the work progressed and made many helpful contributions. I thank her for her scholarship and friendship.

My colleague in interreligious dialogue, Dr. Frank Kaufman of the Interreligious Federation for World Peace, helped me to understand the religious and political dimensions of the Israeli settlements in global context, and I thank him for his insights and deep knowledge.

My friend and colleague, Professor Jonathan Helfand of Brooklyn College, discussed with me many of the issues in this book, and I am grateful for his erudite scholarship and friendship.

Vicky Staufer and Cindy Johnson helped much with the technical preparation of the manuscript, and I thank them for their help and expertise.

Finally, I want to express my deep gratitude to Yetta Marchuck Selengut, my wife and constant conversation partner. She was a careful and perceptive reader and listener, and I want to thank her for her personal encouragement and scholarly contributions.

MAP OF ISRAEL

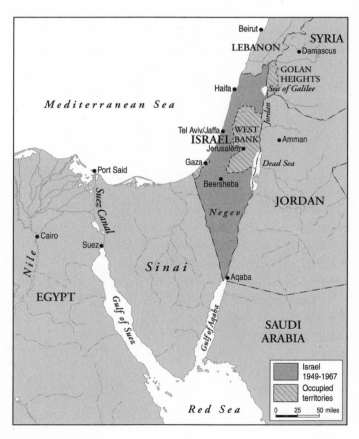

Israel's Borders, 2010

INTRODUCTION

Our Promised Land tells the story of the Israeli settlement movement and shows how a small and marginal but militant group of religious Zionists—calling themselves *Gush Emmunim*, the Bloc of True Believers—was successful in establishing Jewish settlements in the West Bank territories captured by the state of Israel in the 1967 Six-Day War. The Gush Emmunim activists were pious Orthodox Jews, religious fundamentalists who saw the Bible and God's pronouncements as divine truth. For these faithful believers, the divine promises and the covenants between God and the Jewish people as recorded in Jewish scripture are eternally binding the Jewish people to realizing God's plan for divine salvation for all humanity. In this understanding, messianic redemption must and will come when the Jewish people, after long sojourns as a dispersed nation, return to their ancient homeland, to the place the Bible calls *Eretz Yisrael*, the Land of Israel. For these Zionists, messianic redemption truly begins with the establishment of the Jewish state of Israel in 1948. The process continued with what was, in their view, the miraculous victories of the 1967 Six-Day War, when large areas of the biblical Land of Israel, formally under the authority of Egypt, Syria, and Jordan, came under Israeli sovereignty. For these faithful Zionists, the unexpected victory was a clear sign that messianic transformation was really under way and that pious and courageous Jews had a mandate to settle and rule over the entire Land of Israel as they did in biblical times. For the *Yesha* movement, as the early Gush Emmunim came to be known,[1] the newly conquered biblical lands were a divine call for Jews to settle and establish a Jewish commonwealth, based on biblical teachings, over the full Land of Israel. These newly acquired territories were not viewed as conquered or occupied but as Jewish lands, now liberated and returned to their rightful owners in accordance with God's promises to the Jewish people from time immemorial. The Palestinians, having lived for centuries in these areas, similarly see the West Bank lands as their Islamic ancestral home. These opposing religious visions have resulted in ongoing conflict, violence, and war between the two sides and have contributed to international tensions between the West and elements in the Muslim world.

THE DEMAND FOR SETTLEMENT

In the years following the victory in the 1967 war, young, deeply committed religious nationalists, many of them veterans, having served with distinction in the Six-Day War, began agitating for permission from the Israeli government to establish Jewish communities in the newly acquired territories. These young activists were not creating a new or alien religious nationalist ideology or movement. The basic viewpoint of the sacredness of this territory and the legitimacy of Jewish sovereignty over it was and remains an essential element of traditional Jewish theology. What was new was the often militant determination and the new religious justifications for settling land captured in war over which the state of Israel had no formal international rights. The Israeli establishment—the government and military and financial leaders—and public, with few exceptions, were not supportive of settlement in the West Bank territories; instead, they saw these areas as valuable assets to be returned in exchange for a lasting peace with their Arab neighbors. Many traditional Jews also opposed settlement at that time, arguing that settling the full Land of Israel had to wait till the miraculous and supernatural arrival of the Jewish Messiah.

The religious nationalists were not to be deterred. Despite opposition from within Israel and from the international community, the militant settler movement, with the support of their charismatic and innovative rabbinical leadership, was able to begin establishing settlements all over the lands captured in the 1967 war. Beginning with small encampments consisting of a few tents in the late sixties and seventies to establishing moderate-sized cities and towns in Ariel, Efrat, and Kedumim, the settlers transformed the state of Israel. By 2013, there were more than two hundred settlements and an estimated Israeli population of five hundred thousand located in the contested territories. These lands, viewed as an integral and essential Jewish patrimony by the messianic settlers and their supporters, are condemned as an illegal usurpation of occupied territory by the international community and viewed by many as a source of tension between the West and the Islamic world. Despite international diplomatic intervention and multiple United Nations resolutions and peacemaking attempts, the continuing and still growing Israeli settlements in these territories remain an international tinderbox fueling war, murder, and mayhem all over the globe.

The rise of the settler movement is an amazing and an entirely unpredictable story. How did a small, radical religious group on the fringes of Israeli society—a group considered suspect and unworthy by the traditional rabbinical leadership and despised by the secular Zionist leadership and public—achieve such political, demographic, and ideological potency in the twenty-first century? From a position of almost no political power, the settler movement has, by 2014, gained the support of several major parties and well over fifty members of the Israeli parliament, who advocate for the rights of settlers and the legitimacy of their enterprise. This support is not always in full ideological agreement with the religious goals of the movement, but the general mood in the Knesset and in Israeli society as a whole is that the settlers are there to stay. And even if this means standing up to the United States, the country's main military and political patron and ally, and to the objections of the international community, the Israeli government will continue support for the settlement enterprise. International boycotts of Israeli products; violence against settler communities and attacks against Jews and Israelis abroad; and boycotts against Israeli scientists, academics, and artists have not stopped significant Israeli support of the settler movement and its continuing expansion.

MILITANT RELIGIOUS NATIONALISM

The Yesha settler movement represents something highly novel and innovative in Jewish life and history. It is at once deeply religious and messianic and at the same time a worldly movement with distinct territorial and military objectives. It is unalterably opposed to the culture of secular modernity and individualism, but it fully embraces nationalism and has been successful in pursuing its goals within the context of a modern nation-state. The settler movement is theologically grounded in Orthodox Judaism, and its leadership and much of its support come from traditionally observant Jews in Israel and abroad. Traditional Judaism for the last two millennia, however, was passive and nonconfrontational in its relations with governments and with non-Jews. Jews were, in Max Weber's term, the essential "pariah people," always seeking to avoid conflict with outsiders and never wanting to directly challenge governmental authority.[2] Politically and psychologically—and this was theologically justified as well—negotiation, compromise, nonviolence, and acknowledging Jewish political inferiority were the way to interact with the Gentile world. The Yesha movement has therefore revolutionized traditional Jewish religiosity and culture. Today, the movement and its theological leaders proudly proclaim that the time has come for Jews to reject any remnant of pariah mentality or politics and assert their national rights politically, diplomatically, and militarily toward what they see as their rightful homeland, the full Land of Israel as described in Jewish scripture.

The Yesha movement created a new religious Judaism. The former view of the timid Jew, fearful, politically isolated, and dependent on outside protection, has given way to a new Judaism: nationalistic, aggressive, and confrontational. The model of the fearful but wise scholar has been transmuted into the religious Uzi-toting settler, at home and willing to fight and be killed to assert his sovereignty over his ancestral homeland and help realize Jewish destiny. This is certainly nationalism, but a peculiar type of nationalism deeply anchored in Jewish texts and theology. The Yesha movement, as we shall see, has created a new type of religious Judaism, one that has successfully based itself on traditional texts and old rabbinical teachings. Consequently, despite their innovative, even revolutionary, theology and politics, settlers remain an acknowledged and normative part of traditional Orthodox Judaism. The influence of the Yesha movement and its theological teachings has gone far beyond the Jewish community in Israel and has transformed the religious and political outlook of Jews the world over.[3]

During my research and travel for this book, several incidents showed me how the transformation of religious Jewish society was occurring. One summer day, I traveled to the settlement of Ofra, some twenty kilometers from Jerusalem, in the Judean hills. Ofra has been under Israeli control since 1967, and the settlement is known for its dangerous location and as the site of several lethal Palestinian terrorist attacks. I went to Ofra to visit several settler families and to interview a well-known settler leader, Rabbi Avi Gisar, who was also the rabbi of the community and the principal of a residential girls high school that attracts students from all over Israel. At the time of our meeting, the settlement had recently been the scene of several terrorist attacks during which several people traveling to and from the settlement were killed. I had personal experience of the danger of commuting to Ofra, having once been in a convoy when one of the automobiles was shot at and several people were wounded. During my meeting with Rabbi Gisar, I asked, "Aren't you concerned about putting your students in danger? Why set up a school in such a dangerous area?" He thought for a while and carefully responded, "We do all we can to ensure their safety. We give our students a choice: Do they want to be in a place they consider more comfortable? Or do they want be a part of Jewish history, establishing a Jewish presence here and settling and living in the biblical Land of Israel? Given their education, almost all want to be here, knowing that there is a price to returning to our homeland." Here I saw a new Jewish psychology so different from the fearfulness and avoidance of confrontation of the shtetls of eastern Europe, in the Jewish communities in the Muslim Middle East, or even in western European or American Jewish communities, where a sense of homelessness still pervades Jewish society and identity.

In 2008, I went to Hebron, a city sacred to Jews and Muslims, to visit the Jewish community, where about five hundred families live in the midst of an almost all-Arab city of 250,000 Palestinians. I visited a young family with nine children living in a house situated in the midst of a large Palestinian neighborhood. The house had been surreptitiously purchased by the settler community in order to expand the Jewish presence in the city. The local Palestinians, ardent nationalists, were infuriated that the Jewish presence in the town appeared to be expanding. As a result, local militants regularly attacked the house where the family lived. During my visit, I saw some rock throwing and demonstrations by the Palestinians and saw several of the family's children—some preschool aged—running freely about. Although embarrassed, I asked their mother, "Are you not worried about the safety of your children? I know there is conflict here between Israelis and Palestinians, but isn't this conflict a matter for soldiers in battle and not a situation for kids to be involved in? Are you not putting your kids in danger?" Nonplussed, the young mother casually replied, "We are bringing *Geulah*, redemption, and we have to take chances. This is our home and we need to be here. And Hashem [God] will protect us." This was not said in a preaching fashion but rather as a matter of fact, making her comments all the more moving.

Perhaps the most powerful, and terrifying, experience I had that showed the changes I am describing was on a visit to a settlement known for its militancy located deep in the West Bank. The settlement was, at the time, the home of many followers of Rabbi Meir Kahane, the militant Jewish founder of the extremist right-wing nationalist Kach political party. Kahane was assassinated in 1990 by El Sayyid Nosair, an al-Qaeda operative, while speaking in the United States, but some of his most fervent followers lived in the settlement and I was anxious to meet them. Two young Kahane followers picked me up in downtown Jerusalem in an old pickup truck to take me to the settlement, where I would be free to visit and interview members of the group. Both men were wearing a large *kipah* (religious skull cap) and long wool fringes, part of the distinctive garb of religious settlers, and each had a loaded Uzi on his shoulder. This is not unusual, as many settlers carry weapons when entering territories beyond the 1948 armistice line, known as the "Green Line." Shortly after we entered the West Bank areas populated by Palestinians, the young men took off their Uzis and proclaimed, "Let's see if we can fire and frighten the local Arabs." Looking at me, they said, "We need to show that this is Jewish land." I was shocked and frankly terrified, but fortunately, no one was around, no guns were fired, and the trip ended uneventfully.

After reflection and living in the settlements for a time doing participant observation, I understood that these young men and others like them did not see themselves as lawbreakers, nor were they simply mischievous. Instead, this was a renewed Jewish theology in action. This was, I came to realize, religiously motivated activity to achieve messianic goals. What I had read and studied about the settler view of Jewish return to the Holy Land and heard in theological lectures on biblical theology was being enacted with potential violence. No Palestinians appeared that day, and I saw no confrontations. Upon arriving at the settlement, I was warmly welcomed with kind hospitality. When I related my deep concern about this incident with veteran settlement leaders and rabbis, they too were upset and worried and cited many official pronouncements and rabbinical prohibitions against this sort of incitement and potential violence. One rabbi known for his peacemaking efforts spoke for many settlement rabbis when he told me, "These guys are a bunch of crazy, radical nuts, and we can barely control them. They make a lot of trouble for us and give our movement a bad name." Still, as I was leaving, he said these parting words: "We live in a very dangerous neighborhood, and we don't have the luxury of tolerance you have in your middle-class American suburban town." And indeed, as I discovered, the settlements and the settlers were regularly attacked. There are records of hundreds of attacks on settlers, ranging from rock-throwing incidents that result in broken windshields and injury, to random shootings of Jewish travelers on West Bank roads, to murderous attacks in which entire families are killed while asleep in their homes or sitting together at dinner. There are knifings of civilians traveling or shopping, and all settlers know they are living in a hostile and dangerous environment. For many settlers, weapons and retaliation are necessary and legitimate as a means of survival in a threatening environment.[4]

UNDERSTANDING THE SETTLERS

This book tells the story of the settler movement—how it came about and how it was able to transform Jewish religiosity and culture from pariah passivity into militant religious nationalism intent on creating a messianic state in the biblical Land of Israel. The goal is to tell the story of the settlers and present their inside view of the movement in order to shed light on their values, perspectives, and goals and thereby better understand the nature of the continuing Israeli–Palestinian conflict. The settlers' motivations and politics are grounded in religious belief and their task as harbingers of messianic transformation. They see themselves as good and worthy people who are fully dedicated to the Jewish people and to the world at large, even if outsiders refuse to recognize their value and commitment to world transformation. They take the Bible and their holy scriptures as divine truths, and this gives

them potency to persist in a journey leading to world messianic transformation. In this regard, they are truly countercultural. They refuse to
accept Western canons of logic, truth, and democratic politics. They see
Western individualism as rebellion against divine truth. They see separation of religion and state as an illusion fostered on Israel by an assimilated, atheistic, and deracinated secular majority, whom they oppose
and simultaneously wish to win over to God's truth about the role of
Jews in the messianic process. The Israeli secular establishment, along
with most Western Jews, is embarrassed by their theology and faith and
by their refusal to play by modern Western political standards of compromise and secular reasoning. The settlers adopt a religious nationalist
absolutism: God spoke and promised the Jewish people the Land of
Israel; the nation began here, and the Messiah will arrive when all Jews
return to the ancient homeland. Secular politicians who oppose the
settlers talk of demography, a two-state solution, and the danger of
international isolation and the harm it will bring on the economy and
scientific and technological development. This reasoning, however, is
seen by the settlers as a secular and ungodly calculus, for the settlers
have faith that with commitment, sacrifice, and martyrdom God will
surely redeem his chosen children.

This worldview is not readily reconciled with a modern nation-state,
and yet the settler leadership talks about supporting a democratic and
religious Israeli state. Is this possible? Can the state of Israel exist without diplomatic and international legitimacy? Can modern, secular, nonreligious Israelis and messianic orthodox Zionists coexist in a harmonious society? What about non-Jews in the state of Israel? And the real
issue the settlers must face: Can there be peace with their hostile and
recalcitrant neighbors? What about Palestinian rights to a land in which
they have lived for centuries?

The settlers' beliefs, their religious lifestyle, their traditionalist view
of family and gender, their openness to martyrdom, their territorial
aggressiveness, and their rejection of modern Western culture make
them appear strange and dangerous to outsiders in Israel and certainly
to the international community.[5] They challenge the prevailing Western diplomatic assumption that competing national resources, interests,
and goals are at the center of international conflict and violence. As a
consequence of this highly secularized understanding, many diplomats,
academics, and policy analysts want to separate religion from politics

and international conflict and incorrectly imagine that economic aid and development, territorial adjustments, or a rationally imposed order will solve the Middle East conflict. Yesha religious nationalism, as with similar movements in Africa, the Middle East, and Europe, challenges this Western and highly secularized perspective on politics and state-craft. The Yesha movement refuses to separate religion and state; for them, politics and religion are one entity. Sacred history, sacred texts, and the events of thousands of years ago are real and legitimate reasons for staking one's claims to the ancient homeland.

PERSPECTIVES ON THE SETTLER MOVEMENT

This book's approach takes religious nationalist claims, histories, and passions seriously without making judgments about the legitimacy or morality of a particular position. Many works on the Middle East and particularly on the Israeli settlements are avowedly partisan and judg-mental, some in fervent defense, others in militant opposition. This book takes a more neutral, academic view sometimes referred to as value neutrality[6] and seeks to understand the unique confluence of religion, history, and group politics that began and continues to drive the rise of messianic Zionism. The goal in this book is to foster under-standing of the movement and in this way provide a deeper knowledge of the continued Israeli–Palestinian conflict. Though much has been written and spoken on the issue, too often the words, religious motiva-tions, and inner lives of the settlers have been left out. In this book, therefore, I examine their sacred texts and the theological pronounce-ments of their charismatic rabbis and leaders, and I attempt to present the attitudes and passions of the settlers as they spoke with me and as I observed them in their day-to-day lives. Consequently, I have included throughout the book many of their writings and comments gathered in my interviews so that readers will hear the settlers in their own words.

Our Promised Land challenges many misleading assumptions about the Israeli settlement movement. This book demonstrates that the set-tler movement is fully based upon traditional Jewish theology and has the support of the bulk of traditional Jews all around the globe. The settlers have not created a new ideology or religious worldview but have put into practice long-established beliefs and doctrines of rabbinic Judaism. The settlers are aggressive and determined to settle the full biblical Land of Israel, but they are correct in claiming that they have not innovated a new Jewish worldview but are fulfilling in a practical way the doctrines of traditional Judaism. Unless this traditionalism and faith of the settlers are acknowledged, the movement and their power and significance in Israel and the Middle East will be misunderstood and no diplomatic resolution to the conflict will be possible. Diplomats and journalists are befuddled and often erroneous in their coverage and response because they miss the faith and traditionalism of the movement and its acceptance by faithful Jews and Evangelical Christians around the world.

The material for this book was gathered during several years of research between 2011 and 2014, with extended visits to many settlements, participation in religious and cultural events, and formal interviews and conversations with leaders and ordinary residents living in settlement communities. Given my own familiarity and literacy with the biblical and rabbinical literature, which is at the core of the movement's ideology and politics, I read the relevant religious literature, conducted interviews, and had dialogues with the movement's leaders and rabbis. Some of these conversations were information seeking and data gathering, but others were more confrontational, in which I questioned and argued over the legitimacy of the movement's positions given their expressed loyalty to the Talmudic texts. I came away with a respect for the settlers' willingness to talk and open up their communities to my visits and, in general, thought they were frank, honest, and forthright about their beliefs and goals, even where their views are unpopular. Most of the people I met in the movement are convinced that their religious goals would be realized, despite the international pressure against Israel and their settlements. But they are also realistic and politically aware about the unpopularity of their tactics, religiosity, and political program.

THE PLAN OF THE BOOK

I begin the story in chapter 1 by discussing the emergence of the Yesha settler movement amid the dramatic events and euphoric mood in Israel after its victory in the Six-Day War. Although Jewish settlement in the captured territories was wholly unexpected, and actually opposed by Israeli military and political elites, the religious settlers' determination, coupled with their innovative diplomatic and militant strategies, overcame this opposition and established a successful political and religious movement building settlements all over the West Bank and Gaza. Chapter 2 discusses the settlers' transformation of political Zionism from a secular nationalism to a fundamentalist religious nationalism promoting messianic world transformation. This worldview required new communal, religious, and ideological support, and chapter 3 discusses the development of a new and highly innovative culture and theology legitimating the new religious Zionist nationalism. Chapter 4 takes us inside the settlement world and gives an ethnographic view of the settlements and describes some of my visits and interviews with settlement rabbis, leaders, and ordinary people. This chapter uses interview material so readers can hear the settlers in their own words. The Israeli settlements are at the center of Middle East turmoil, conflict, and violence, and chapter 5 considers the future of the settlement enterprise. The settlers see themselves as faithful Bible believers who have full rights to the entire biblical Land of Israel. But the Palestinian people, given their scripture and traditions, claim a similar right to those lands, which they consider their Muslim inheritance. What of the future? Can these religious claims be reconciled?

There are many foreign terms used in this book, and a glossary is provided to explain and give context to these terms. Key figures in the movement are listed and their importance explained in the section on "Key Figures." A map of the areas discussed in this book is also included. "A Note on Methods" is appended for those wanting more information on research methods and data collection.

I

THE RISE OF THE SETTLEMENTS

JUDAISM AND THE LAND OF ISRAEL

From the time of their emergence as a unique religion and nation, the Jewish people have considered the Land of Israel, Eretz Yisrael, their national homeland promised to them by God, as recorded in the Hebrew Bible.[1] The pivotal and defining events of Jewish history have taken place in the Land of Israel. The stories of the patriarchs; the narratives of the ancient prophets; the tales of wars with Israel's enemies, the machinations of kings and despotic tyrants, and the internecine Jewish battles between those faithful to the monotheistic Jewish deity and those who sought refuge in idolatry and paganism—all take place in the Land of Israel. The ancient Jewish religious center, the *Beit Hamikdash*, the beautiful, elaborate, and sacred Temple where prayers and animal sacrifices took place daily, was located on the Temple Mount in Jerusalem, an area still sacred to world Jewry. Even during those historic periods when Jerusalem and Judea were under foreign domination, Jews remained in the Land of Israel, and those who resided in the surrounding areas returned to worship and offer sacrifices at the Temple. Jews saw themselves as God's chosen people, a nation and a religion with a national homeland and a sacrificial center linking them with the one true deity.

The central and most traumatic event transforming Jewish life, religion, and culture occurred in the year 70 AD, when under Roman attack, the Temple was destroyed. In the years following, Jews were expelled from the Land of Israel, and the Jewish homeland was renamed Palestine in an effort to erase its connection to the Jews. These events, known as *Churban Bayit*, the destruction of the Temple house, cast the Jews into exile as a defeated people dispersed throughout the Middle East, North Africa, and Europe, and the day the invading Roman army entered the Temple grounds is still commemorated by Jews today with fasting and mourning. The expulsion and "exile," as these events came to be known, entirely transformed Jewish culture, religiosity, and politics. From a nation certain of its identity and destiny, willing to do battle for God and the homeland, the Jews became an unwelcome pariah people at the mercy of host countries. In the ensuing centuries, in both Muslim and Christian lands, the Jews were seen as a strange and alien group and were often the subject of prejudice and persecution, forced to live in ghettos and restricted from owning land or engaging in certain occupations and professions. Still, throughout this two-thousand-year exile, Jewish communities remained in the Land of Israel, and Jews all over the globe continued their attachment and loyalty to their ancient homeland. The prayer "Next year in Jerusalem" was recited at every family seder meal, and special daily prayers were instituted to remember the Roman defeat and expulsion and assert the eventual return to the Holy Land. These memories and liturgies commemorated and institutionalized the connection between Jews and the Land of Israel, but they were just that: words, prayers, liturgical songs, with no activity or program to realize a return to the ancestral homeland. Jews would faithfully recite, "Next year in Jerusalem . . . ," but their life and work was in Kiev, Cordoba, or Marrakesh. The yearning for the return to the biblical homeland was authentic but remained focused on prayer and faith, with no political goal or action.[2]

POLITICAL ZIONISM AND THE EMERGENCE OF A JEWISH STATE

The modern Zionist movement, beginning in the nineteenth century, profoundly changed Jewish political and religious passivity. Zionism, influenced by the emerging European nationalisms, called for the return of Jews to their homeland in Palestine and began a practical program of migration, settlement, and the establishment of a modern Jewish state in the biblical Land of Israel. The Zionist movement refused to accept a pariah status for Jews, asking, even demanding, that the international community provide a homeland for the dispersed Jews. The central and leading figure in the new Zionist movement was Theodor Herzl, a Viennese journalist and playwright who was an assimilated and not at all a religious Jew, but who nonetheless argued that Jews were an alien and despised people in foreign lands and that the unhappy plight of the Jews could only be solved with the establishment of their own modern nation-state. The Zionist movement was a curious amalgam of highly secular Jews, who were more motivated by the budding nationalism of the late nineteenth and early twentieth centuries than by divine promises, and religious Orthodox Jews, who saw the movement as a religious enterprise enabling Jews to return to their ancestral home as a prelude to eventual messianic events.

The Zionist movement began slowly but by the early twentieth century was able to successfully settle tens of thousands of Jews in Palestine and gained the support of millions of Jews all over the world. The avowed goal was clear: to obtain by international consent a Jewish homeland under Jewish sovereignty. This was not an easy task. Palestinian Arabs had lived in the land for centuries, and they too considered this their territory and saw Jewish Zionist settlers as interlopers who with international backing were taking over their national property. Conflict, violence, and attacks were common throughout the early twentieth century between the now growing Jewish population and the Arab Palestinians. After World War I and the dissolution of the Ottoman Empire, the governance of Palestine was given over to Great Britain under a League of Nations mandate to divide the territory between the two warring parties. There were a series of international meetings in an attempt to settle the ongoing and increasingly violent dispute and broker a compromise, but nothing worked. [3]

World War II and the European Holocaust, in which six million Jews were murdered, accelerated migration to Palestine and convinced European governments that a national home for the Jewish people was necessary. The Zionists successfully asserted their view that the Jews were unwelcome on foreign soil and that a national home was the only way to ensure their safety and well-being. After much diplomatic negotiation between representatives of the Jewish and Arab communities, and because of the impossibility of establishing a pluralistic binational state, a partition plan organized and approved by the United Nations was put into effect. The biblical Land of Israel was divided between Jews and Arabs. One state, which became Israel, received the Mediterranean coastal area and southern terrain, while the portion allotted to the Arab state was to be created from the West Bank and the areas surrounding Jerusalem and the northern areas of the ancient Land of Israel. There were other adjustments as well, with Jerusalem to be an international city open to all.[4]

To the negotiating diplomats, this seemed a fair and rational conclusion to the conflict between Jews and Arabs. But this was the Middle East, a place where historical and religious memory is alive and never to be forgotten, and both sides were unhappy. The Jews considered the whole of the Land of Israel their ancestral place, and the Palestinians living in the land understood Palestine to be their rightful home. Nonetheless, the Jewish community went along with the partition, and the then head of the Palestinian Jewish community and later the first prime minister of Israel, David Ben-Gurion, proclaimed in May 1948 the establishment of a Jewish state in those parts of biblical Israel allotted to the Jews. The Palestinian community and the wider Muslim world refused to accept the partition plan, and the first of several wars and battles between to the two sides began in 1947 after the announcement of the partition. An armistice agreement but not a permanent peace was reached in 1949, after many bloody battles and with the new Jewish state annexing additional territory not granted in the original partition.

CONFLICT BETWEEN ARABS AND JEWS

Palestinian Arabs and the worldwide Muslim community saw the partition agreement and the establishment of a Jewish commonwealth, even only in portions of Palestine, as an encroachment on Muslim sacred soil. For Islam, Palestine was Muslim territory, *Dar al-Islam*, the site of the Al-Aqsa mosque, which has great prominence in Muslim religiosity, and had been under Muslim jurisdiction for centuries. For many in the Islamic world, Israel was an illegitimate state foisted on the Muslim world by a powerful and uncaring West. The new state was not to be recognized diplomatically, nor would any economic or cultural interactions take place. All means of opposition, including armed attacks, were acceptable against the nascent Jewish state. There could be no coming to terms with the newly created country. The state of Israel needed to be eliminated.[5]

The Jewish community had a more complex and ambivalent response. Jews in Palestine and most of the rest of the world were euphoric over the establishment a Jewish state that could take in hundreds of thousands of concentration camp survivors and displaced persons. The Jewish people had now returned to their ancient homeland after the long two-thousand-year exile. Hebrew became the official language, Jewish holidays would be the official state holidays, and Jews from anywhere in the world would have a safe haven and be welcomed as citizens. Once a dispersed, weak people herded into death camps, the Jews were now to have their own country, their own language, and above all their own armed forces ready to defend Jews and Judaism. And yet, particularly for religious Zionists and for Jewish nationalists of all types, much was missing. The essence of the Zionist goal and program called for the establishment of a Jewish state in biblical Israel, and this did not happen with the partition plan. Ancient sacred Jerusalem and the holy ground of the Temple and the Western Wall in Jerusalem where Jews had prayed for centuries were now under Jordanian control. The Tomb of the Patriarchs, the final resting place of Abraham, Isaac, and Jacob, was in Hebron, closed to Jews and under foreign sovereignty. The hills and deserts of Judea and the mountainous terrain of Samaria, places where Jewish history took place, where prophets spoke and kings fought and farmers tilled the land, were still under foreign domination. This lack was felt if not always articulated by the new Israeli citizenry. The jubilation, the relief from victimhood, and the realization of a homeland suppressed, for most, the price of the compromise and the loss of the historic land.

Still, religious memory and sacred history do not easily disappear. One religious sage, Rabbi Tzvi Yehuda Kook, who was to become the mentor and charismatic leader of the settler Yesha movement, gave voice to this continuing yearning for the wholeness of the Zionist vision. Kook recounted that on the day in May 1948 when the state of Israel was proclaimed, he was deeply distressed, morose, and could not participate in the festival atmosphere and celebrations. In his words, "I could not go to dance in the streets because I felt that I like the Land of Israel had been cut into pieces and wounded in my heart." He recounted to his students that the partition "divided my Land" and severed the Jewish connection of so many places sacred to Jews. And he complained about the easy acceptance of the plan and the loss of the many historic and sacred places long revered by Jews. And so he insisted, "Where is our Hebron? Did we forget about this? And where is our Shechem? Did we forget about this? Where is our Jericho? Did we forget about this too? And where is our other side of the Jordan? And where is each block of earth? Each part of Hashem's land."[6]

Kook's religious yearnings and nationalist goals were not on the political or cultural agenda of the new Jewish state. Physical survival, economic progress, and international recognition were the main concerns. This is not to say that Israelis and Zionist Jews worldwide were unaware of the loss of crucial parts of the ancient homeland. For many religious and right-wing Zionists, the new state was but the beginning of a process that would in time lead to the establishment of a Jewish state on both sides of the Jordan. This view was, however, at the time and until 1967, a distinctly minority and unpopular position. As a matter of fact, the fifties and early sixties saw a real acceptance in Israeli society of the territorial division, and with the rising tide of secularization and the socialist Labor party at the helm of the government, talk of a greater Israel and messianism was muted. Still, quietly and out of sight of the secular establishment, religious fundamentalist nationalists, in their schools, youth groups, literature, and the seminary *yeshivoth*, were agitating for an expansionist and religious messianic agenda for the state. Until 1967, these ideas and programs were limited to religious sectarian groups who had little or no power or cultural standing. Most Israelis found them irrelevant and viewed them as extremists or religious fanatics. All this changed with the 1967 Six-Day War.

THE 1967 SIX-DAY WAR

The Arab–Israeli war in 1967 entirely transformed the state of Israel, the Jewish religion, and the psychology of Jews all over the world. In the months and weeks before the war, a blockade against ships destined for Israel's ports was enforced by the Egyptian Navy and Arab armies were massed around Israel's borders. The Egyptian Army was poised to attack from the south, Syrian forces were readying on the northern border, and Jordanian forces were prepared to attack the Jewish sections of Jerusalem. The goal of the attack, as expressed throughout the Arab and Muslim world, was to destroy the Jewish state and remake Palestine, which in their view had been unjustly taken from Arab authority in 1948. The Israelis and indeed Jews throughout the world feared that the coming attack would lead to another Holocaust, the mass murder of Jews, and the destruction of the relatively new Jewish state. Prayer meetings were held in Jewish communities all over the world, and thousands of young Jews from around the world left their homes and careers to go to Israel and fight in the coming war or work as civilian volunteers. In Israel itself, preparations were made for the expected massive casualties, and trauma centers were set up all over the country. Gravesites were dug in civilian parks to accommodate the thousands expected to be killed. The state feared for its very existence, and, as the historian Tom Segev put it, an apocalyptic mood enveloped the entire country.[7]

Things turned out very differently. In the opening days of the war, the Israeli Air Force in a preemptive attack destroyed the entire Egyptian Air Force and within days occupied the Gaza district and the Sinai Desert. The West Bank was taken from Jordanian authority, the strategic Golan Heights were taken from Syria, and, after fierce fighting with elite Jordanian forces, the Old City of Jerusalem came under Israeli authority. The reunification of the city of Jerusalem with its many sacred sites (from 1948 until the Israeli victory, Jews had been forbidden entry to the Old City) was particularly important since the Jews had claimed Jerusalem as their ancient and sacred capital and the lack of Jewish presence there had been particularly demoralizing to Israelis and Jews all over the world. By the conclusion of the war, the territory under Israeli control had doubled, and millions of formally Jordanian, Egyptian, and Syrian citizens were now living under Israeli authority. The territory gained in the war not only gave Israel room for expansion and in some cases control over oil reserves and other natural resources but restored Israeli control over what Jews believed were ancient and sacred Jewish sites. Most important, in the religious Zionist view, was the return to Jewish authority of the Old City of Jerusalem, including the old Jewish Quarter and the Western Wall, the last remaining part of the ancient Jewish Temple, Beit Hamikdash. The war also gave Jews control over and access to the ancient city of Hebron and its Tomb of the Patriarchs, the Gush Etzion region populated by Jews until the 1948 war, and a whole host of ancient biblical sites all over the West Bank.

The military victory was clear and extraordinary. The people of Israel and Jews around the globe were relieved, overjoyed, and emboldened. But the victory and territorial expansion brought their own ambivalences and anxieties. How did it happen that a small, somewhat underdeveloped country not even twenty years from independence was able to defeat the combined Arab armies with the support of Muslim allies worldwide? Jews for the last two thousand years lived a diaspora existence as a despised and pariah people, without a land of their own, without political or military power, and now this same people stigmatized for their vulnerability had emerged as a military power and, in the view of much of the world, an aggressive conqueror ruling over other peoples and denying them national rights. Jews for millennia had conceived of themselves as victims of alien governmental and military power—the European Holocaust had ended only some twenty-three years earlier—and had little historical experience with military victory, political power, or occupation. Despite the relief and joy of the military success, some Israeli theologians and political thinkers expressed shame and embarrassment at the overwhelming victory and subsequent occupation of Arab land. Perhaps, some argued, the preemptive war was the result of a Jewish overreaction fueled by the trauma of the recent Holocaust. Perhaps greater restraint and peacemaking would have avoided a war. Most Israelis, however, saw the victory as heralding a new era in which Jews "never again" would be passive victims. The soul-searching and political controversy over the meaning and response to the 1967 victory divided Israeli society—and continues to do so—and coalesced around three political and theological responses: (1) the secular political perspective, (2) the traditional religious perspective, and (3) the religious nationalist perspective.

The predominantly secular Israeli view was that the war was necessary but that no religious or theological meaning could be given to the victory. It was the consequence of good military planning and the weakness and unpreparedness of the enemy. The war meant that Israel and the Jewish people had come of age and were now a normal nation that could defend itself. The military victory meant that serious negotiations with the Arab neighbors involving territorial exchanges could now take place so that a full peace agreement could be signed. The idea behind this thinking was that now the neighboring countries saw Israeli power and would be ready to make peace. In this view, Israel and the Jews were to become a "normal" country, ready to take part in political and diplomatic bargaining.[8]

RELIGIOUS RESPONSES TO THE 1967 VICTORY

The traditionally religious population saw the victory as something more. That a small, besieged nation could triumph over the combined Arab world and retake the sacred precincts of Jerusalem and the Temple area meant that something extraordinary had taken place, something akin to events in the Hebrew Bible. This was no ordinary military victory but the work of divine power; God, as the guardian of his people, had intervened to save the "remnant of Israel" after the Holocaust. This extraordinary event saved the Jewish people from destruction and enabled them to continue to be loyal and faithful to their religious traditions and teachings. The victory did not change anything about Jews, Judaism, or the situation of Jews in the world. True, a great, even legendary victory had taken place, but the Jews and Israel were still in a precarious position, living in a world that still harbored hatred for them, and it would be best to remain cautious, defensive, and even mistrusting in relations with the Gentile world. Put differently, the victorious war was a welcome sign of God's mercy—as indeed had occurred previously in Jewish history—but the events should not change traditional Jewish theological passivity and messianic waiting. One German-born American ultra-Orthodox rabbi, Simon Schwab, expressed his relief over the victory but cautioned his congregants not to give great significance to the events: "Nothing has changed, we are in *Golus* [Exile] as we have been for two thousand years."[9]

For religious Zionist nationalists, everything had changed; the miraculous 1967 victory was a divine call to the Jewish people. In this view, the victory and reunification of Jerusalem and Israeli control of the Temple Mount and areas of the West Bank, known to Jews as biblical Judea and Samaria, were truly miraculous and the unfolding of the messianic age foretold in Jewish scripture. This was no mere military victory or even a divine action simply to save Jews from destruction. This victory and the retaking of Jewish lands and sacred sites was unprecedented, a divine prophetic message to the Jewish people, which demanded a quantum change in Jewish theology and psychology. The Jews could no longer be passive actors in history, they were no longer to be victims of other nations or empires, and most significantly, the religious apocalyptic passivity that was the hallmark of Jewish theology for over two thousand years had to be abandoned. This was God's call to his people to wake up, seize power, and rule over all of Eretz Yisrael. This victory meant that the ordinary politics of diplomacy and the give and take of international relations no longer applied. The dream of secular Zionism for normalcy, to be like all other nations, was apostasy and the denial of Jewish destiny. God's call now was to settle the whole of biblical Israel and have all Jews immigrate to the Jewish state and establish a religious commonwealth over the full territories of biblical Israel governed by Jewish religious law, Halacha. In this way, the messianic age could arrive and bring about the end of days described in Jewish and Christian scripture. All this would come about—that was certain—but it was dependent upon Jewish courage, fearlessness, and faith and the willingness to sacrifice and be martyrs in this sacred mission.

At first this messianic response to the war was a distinctly minority view. It was followed by some activist Zionist rabbis and students of the Merkaz Harav Yeshiva headed by Rabbi Tzvi Yehuda Kook, who had always maintained the rights of Jews to the whole of biblical Israel and who saw in the pre-1967 boundaries an abandonment of Jewish destiny. Rabbi Kook was a unique rabbinical figure. He was the son of Rabbi Avraham Hakohen Kook, the former chief rabbi of the Jewish community in Palestine, who was a famed cabalist and a renowned Talmudic scholar who had studied in traditionalist European yeshivas but had rejected their anti-Zionism, arguing that Jewish settlement in the Land of Israel was religiously obligatory and was the prelude to messianic redemption.[10] The elder Kook was a much-beloved figure in pre-state Palestine, a traditionalist rabbi who embraced all Jews, secular and religious, claiming that even the most unobservant were engaged in a sacred mission of messianic redemption. His son, Rabbi Tzvi Yehudah, though dressed in the black garb of a traditionalist rabbi, similarly rejected traditional rabbinical religious and political passivity and elaborated his father's theology, giving it a practical political agenda. The younger Kook encouraged and gave a rabbinical imprimatur to settlers and is rightly seen as the father of the Yesha movement. In what has come to be seen as a prescient, even prophetic, pronouncement, just prior to the Six-Day War, Kook bemoaned during the May 1967 Independence Day celebrations at his yeshiva the loss of biblical land in the 1948 partition and chastised his students for not being sufficiently mournful over the division of biblical Israel. "They divided my Land," he cried out, and he refused to fully join in the joyous Independence Day festivities.[11] The subsequent reclaiming of the city of Jerusalem and occupation of the Judean and Samarian regions by the Israeli military just a month later came to be seen as a vindication of the old sage's religious prayers. Well before the 1967 victory, Kook and his followers saw the state of Israel as the beginning of messianic redemption, and the victory and occupation to them were a further and more certain divine assurance that Jews must settle all the territories of biblical Israel and lay the groundwork for a messianic world transformation. The 1967 victory was for them a divine call—even demand—for the faithful to establish Jewish sovereignty over all the lands and inhabitants of the biblical territory of ancient Israel.

Messianic interpretations of the 1967 victory were, however, rejected by most secular and religious elements in Israeli society. The war was a military victory that resulted in greater security and was seen as the basis for land exchanges that could finally end hostilities between Arabs and Israelis. True, the lands of biblical Israel were part of Jewish history and even places of modern Jewish settlement until the 1948 war, but compromises had to be made in accordance with the 1948 partition agreement. For the Israeli public, talk of messianism and restoring biblical kingdoms or using the Bible as a guide to politics was dangerous and could only exacerbate tensions with Arab neighbors and retard attempts at a comprehensive peace settlement. The messianists were seen as outlandish zealots, religious fundamentalists who were spouting mystical doctrines that had no place in a modern democratic state. The messianic view, however, despite its oddness and the discomfort it brought to most Israelis, had a solid basis in Jewish texts and rabbinical traditions. Indeed, the official prayer adopted by the state rabbinate to be used in synagogue liturgy shortly after independence reflected this view, claiming that the nascent state was the "beginning of messianic redemption."[12] This text was the creation of an older generation of Zionist rabbis who were strong believers in messianic redemption. To them, composing the prayer at the dawn of the new state, the liturgical phrases were poetic longings, deep religious wishes, but they did not view their text as a program for political annexation, settlement, and military action. To these rabbis, the creation of the state of Israel was a fulfillment of biblical promises, but they saw the new country as a fragile entity dependent on the goodwill of the United States and western Europe, and any talk of messianism and settlement in Arab territories would lead to sanctions and threaten the existence of the Jewish state. They could not deny that the establishment of the state had messianic dimensions, but they saw this as irrelevant to the political situation in which the small state found itself. For these Zionist rabbis, messianic thinking and politics had a real basis in Judaism and in the new Jewish state, but this was for the future, when the state would be powerful and self-sufficient. Even more strongly opposed to messianic rhetoric and politics were the ultra-Orthodox Haredim, who opposed the entire Zionist movement and viewed Zionist talk of messianism as outright heresy. For the Haredim, all a pious Jew can do is wait patiently and faithfully for divine, supernatural messianic transformation. They believed the messianic followers of Rabbi Kook were dangerous and threatening to traditional Judaism—they looked like strictly Orthodox Jews, were deeply knowledgeable in rabbinic literature, and followed strict family modesty taboos, but they refused to accept the passivity and apocalyptic stance that typified Haredi Judaism. The terrible illusion of Kook and his followers, in the Haredi view, was their belief that human activity could change Jewish destiny and hasten messianic transformation.[13]

GUSH EMMUNIM AND THE RISE OF THE SETTLEMENTS

Despite the ideological and political opposition of most Israelis to the settlement program of Kook and his followers, the nascent settler movement and its then named Gush Emmunim—Bloc of True Believers—were able to establish a successful organizational and economic infrastructure to place settlements, towns, and small cities throughout the West Bank. The Gush Emmunim were primarily Orthodox Jewish yeshiva students or graduates of yeshivas, often veterans of the Six-Day War who, together with their wives and in many cases their children, left their homes in cities in Israel to settle in the newly conquered territory. This settlement activity began slowly, at first in areas adjacent to Jerusalem and later throughout all areas of the Palestinian West Bank, and today has mushroomed to over 120 settlements with over five hundred thousand people.[14] These settlements vary in size and structure. They include small illegal outposts populated by fervent messianists but also well-established suburban communities like Kedumim in the Samarian mountains, which has a large professional middle-class population, and small cities like Ariel in the Samaria region with its own highly regarded university. The rise of these settlements and cities in Palestinian areas was an entirely unpredictable development. A small, almost cultlike religious minority in the early years of the state, against official Israeli policy, against the entire international community, and even opposed by their own Orthodox coreligionists, were able to establish communities all over the West Bank.

The Arab communities, understandably, saw the intrusion of Jewish settlers into these Palestinian areas as a direct threat to their autonomy and state-building activities. The Palestinian leadership understood that these Jewish communities were carefully and strategically placed all over the length and breadth of the Palestinian areas to make it difficult to establish a viable future Palestinian state. The settlement building was also strongly opposed by the Israeli elite. Leading Israeli intellectuals, artists, politicians, and most educated Israelis were opposed to the settlement enterprise, seeing it as an impediment to peace and an illegal and immoral undertaking.[15] Still, despite the serious opposition, the settlement enterprise continued, and as time went on the numbers of Israelis supporting it increased and a growing number of families wanted to reside in these new communities. It appears that the settlers tapped the long-repressed Jewish desire for sovereignty and messianic redemption. For many Israelis, the settlers may have been somewhat strange for wanting to live in a hostile environment, religious zealots and violent revolutionaries, but they were also faithful and avant-garde pioneers who were willing to sacrifice personal needs to establish Jewish life over the whole of biblical Israel. The settlers' religiosity, faithfulness, and martyrdom came to be seen as a testament to the continuing power of Jewish belief that after two thousand years of homelessness the Jewish people would return and reclaim their historic right to their ancestral home.[16]

RELIGION, POLITICS, AND THE RISE OF THE
ISRAELI SETTLEMENTS

The building of Jewish settlements in the West Bank—or in Judea and Samaria, as the settlers refer to the area by its biblical names—is a complicated story of Israeli ambivalence; settlers faced official governmental disapproval and informal encouragement. Israelis felt a historical and spiritual longing for the biblical lands coupled with an awareness that the settlements would lead to war, conflict, and international condemnation. The initial Israeli hope was to broker a deal with King Hussein of Jordan in which virtually all the West Bank would be returned in exchange for peace. In a secret memo prepared shortly after the war for the prime minister's office, Israeli experts advised that the captured land be immediately returned or Israel would be seen as a colonial state—just as colonialism was vanishing and being condemned internationally. Moreover, the memo warned, annexing or continued occupation would endanger Israel's Jewish identity by taking on a population of well over a million and a half Arab Palestinians. It appears that the memo's recommendation was welcomed by the Israeli government, but the Jordanian king delayed any agreement, and his refusal to commit to a public peace treaty for fear of alienating his fellow Arab leaders made this arrangement impossible in the immediate postwar period.[17]

Still, the idea to return the captured lands in exchange for a peace agreement remained strong in Israeli diplomatic circles. Levi Eshkol, the Israeli prime minister at the time, understood the dilemma facing Israel and urged delay in taking any unilateral action, hoping that over time a deal could be struck with Jordan that would give Arab West Bank Palestinians some degree of autonomy in union with the Hashemite kingdom in Jordan while retaining a Jewish presence in all of Jerusalem and in other holy places in the West Bank. The most popular version of this approach was formulated by the prominent Israeli general Yigal Allon—the "Allon Plan" still referred to in some policy circles[18] —in which Israel would annex most of the strategic Jordan Valley, East Jerusalem, and the former Jewish Etzion bloc while immediately ceding to Jordan the Arab-populated areas of the West Bank. Arabs living in the new Israeli areas would receive Israeli citizenship so that no official discrimination would exist, and only one governmental system would apply to both Jews and Arab Palestinians. The plan had a lot of popular appeal to moderates on both sides. It was a reasonable and rational compromise, but this was the Middle East, and the Jordanians and the Palestinians immediately rejected it as appropriating Arab lands (King Hussein believed he would be assassinated by Islamic militants if he agreed to the plan), and nationalist Israelis similarly rejected it out of hand. For the Israeli right wing, the Allon Plan was treasonous and heretical; all of the West Bank and Judea, including the sacred city of Hebron and all the places of ancient biblical settlement, had to remain in Israeli hands, and moreover, the nationalists argued, it would be suicidal to surrender this strategic territory to mortal enemies. The reality was that no one wanted an agreement—not the Arab states, not the Palestinians, and not the Israelis. Perhaps had the Arab states agreed to a territorial compromise, Palestinian nationalists might have gone along and the possibility of peace would have encouraged the Israeli establishment to cede land won in battle. As it was, the political and military deadlock and the absence of realistic possibilities for a territorial compromise further emboldened the messianic elements in Israel.[19]

The 1967 victory had unleashed such euphoria in Israel and in world Jewry that an immediate return to the pre-1967 borders was unwelcome to most Israelis. Israel was a transformed country. "Ecstasy" and a sense of invincibility was the mood of the day. All elements in the society, secular and religious, rich and poor, Middle Eastern and European, appeared caught up in the excitement as history was being made and historical wrongs were to be made right. The Jews and their infant state of Israel were making history and were the rulers of their ancient lands, having to answer to no one. Moderate establishment politicians like the future Israeli prime minister and 1973 Nobel Peace Prize–winner Shimon Peres, questioned by journalists about settling in the heartland of Samaria amid a Palestinian population, claimed that settlements could be set up anywhere and refused to oppose them. Moshe Dayan, the much-decorated Arabic-speaking general known for his sensitivity to Arab culture, was opposed to officially annexing the territories but still insisted on holding on to much of the captured land. Let's "just shut up and rule" was his position, a not unusual view in the postwar period.[20]

In this situation, there was no political will to cede territory even among the moderate political and military establishment. The leftist socialist Mapam party was the notable exception in advocating immediate return of the captured lands. Some leftist intellectuals, artists, and diplomats, such as the novelist Amos Oz and Abba Eban, the Israeli representative to the United Nations, warned of the hostile response of the international community over possible annexation, but they too expressed joy and announced their attachment to the biblical lands. Their opposition to settlements at the time was practical and political. They opposed settlements but still identified with the attachment to the ancient lands. Even some leading stalwarts of the secular socialist left, Israelis who had championed coexistence with the Palestinians, had a change of heart when it came to the ancient biblical territory. Despite their strong secularism and even rabid atheism, their outlook and rhetoric became increasingly religiously poetic. Moshe Shamir, a leading novelist associated with the Mapam socialist left, talked about the divine nature of the victory. All of a sudden, religious language and biblical images appeared in his writings. A secularist who wanted no infusion of religion in state affairs, a cosmopolitan writer and intellectual far removed from messianic religiosity, Shamir compared the Israeli victory and particularly the capture of the Temple Mount to God's revelation at Sinai. As one Israeli commentator put it, "all that he had formally expected from Marx and Stalin was on the cusp of fulfillment." Natan Alterman, the unofficial Israeli poet laureate and also a leftist secularist who in the past had opposed state intrusion in religion, had a change of heart and saw the victory as demanding that Israelis hold on to the West Bank, which he called the "cradle of the nation," and urged settlement in the new territories.[21] The Israeli right-wing parties under the leadership of Menachem Begin, who later became prime minister, had always been opposed to the 1948 partition of Palestine. They were especially supportive of settlement. Until the 1967 victory, they were political and ideological outcasts; their view of holding on to all of biblical Israel was in the eyes of the ruling socialist parties ridiculous, immoral, and dangerous. But now their much-maligned view became a legitimate voice in the public debate. What had sounded like religious fanaticism on the political fringe became a realistic political option. The religious Zionist followers of Rabbi Tzvi Yehuda Kook now had popular sentiment on their side. Reality had gone their way.

In this situation of national and religious ecstasy, moral and political ambivalence, and the inability of Arab leaders to broker a deal with the

Israelis, the groups most infused with religious and nationalist desire to settle the new lands in the West Bank and Gaza were able to prevail upon the still somewhat recalcitrant establishment to give permission and provide the absolutely necessary financial and military aid to settle parts of the newly obtained territory. The acquiescence of state authorities was essential to building settlements. This does not mean that state authorities would have necessarily built these settlements and towns in the West Bank on their own initiative, but when presented with a determined nationalistic and highly committed cadre and given the victorious mood and failure to find any viable peace partner, state authorities knowingly cooperated, and at times were outwitted and hoodwinked, in aiding and supporting the settlement enterprise. The messianic cadres, fervent followers of Rabbi Tzvi Yehuda Kook, were no simpletons hooked on land grabbing but a group fully attuned to Jewish history and Israeli psychology and with a strategic plan for settlement that found a measure of acceptance among elements of the Israeli establishment.

GUSH ETZION: THE CHILDREN RETURN

The first of the settlements to be built on land captured in the 1967 war was in the Judean mountains, directly south of Jerusalem and Bethlehem in an area known as Gush Etzion, the Etzion bloc. Prior to the establishment of the Israeli state, this area had seen several successful Jewish agricultural settlements on land purchased from local Palestinians in the 1920s and 1930s, and Jews considered it a Jewish area. During the 1948 battles, Jordanian forces attacked the villages, overwhelmed their military defenses, and captured and destroyed all the settlements, with hundreds of Jewish villagers killed during the hostilities. Those taken into captivity were not released to Israeli authorities for years. The loss of the Etzion settlements was a particular trauma for the Jewish community. The remaining survivors from their expulsion in 1948 kept the memory of the loss in the public eye, holding yearly memorial services and keeping alive the memory and shame of the defeat. There were stories in Israeli newspapers of survivors and their children standing on Jerusalem rooftops gazing at the remains of the destroyed villages in the distant hills. Remembering the loss of the Etzion villages became part of the collective memory of the nascent

Jewish state. Consequently, after the 1967 victory and the retaking of
the West Bank, the former residents and their survivors appealed to
have their former settlements reestablished in the retaken Etzion bloc.
This did not come easy. Israeli archives of the discussions leading up to
granting rights to the survivor families to return show Levy Eshkol, the
prime minister at the time, sympathetic to the survivors but still deeply
fearful that the settlement activity would impede an eventual peace
agreement and bring about international condemnation. The mood of
the country, the sense of victory, and the persistence of the survivors
convinced the government to grant permission to reestablish a community surrounding the new yeshiva talmudical academy in the Etzion
region. Finally, in September 1968 the permission to build was granted,
giving the new settlers a small portion of land and permission for only a
small number of residences in the area of the Talmudical school.

This was not an entirely unpopular decision. Even opponents of the
occupation went along with settling in the Etzion region, reasoning that
Jewish settlements had been there decades before the establishment of
the Jewish state. The permission to settle the Etzion bloc was not, they
reasoned, settling the West Bank and creating a greater Israeli state.
Those in the forefront of settling the Etzion bloc, however, were fervent religious Zionists who saw the return to the Etzion region as just
the beginning of Jewish settlement over the whole of biblical Israel.
One of the leaders of the new settlement, Hanan Porat, an ordained
rabbi and fervent follower of the messianic religious politics of Rabbi
Kook, as well as a much-decorated paratrooper, articulated the often
unspoken agenda of the new settlers when he proclaimed that the new
settlement had "redeemed" Jewish land that was now returned to its
rightful owners. For the Etzion settlers, the return to Gush Etzion was
not a real estate deal but an event of cosmic proportions fulfilling biblical prophecies of a Jewish return. The settling of the Etzion bloc was a
watershed event as it legitimated settlement in territory captured in the
1967 war, land that was earlier ceded to Arab authority in the 1948
armistice agreement. The state authorities who supported the new settlers thought they were righting a historical wrong and an earlier expulsion by enabling refugees and war heroes—Porat was one such hero—
to return, and some Israeli military analysts even saw the Etzion bloc
functioning as a protective cordon for the city of Jerusalem. The religious Zionist settlers, however, saw the new settlement as opening the

door for state permission for expansion throughout Judea and Samaria. Here in the settling of the Etzion bloc can be seen the future strategy of messianic Zionism. The new and returning settlers had a clear expansionist messianic ideology, but they knew that the Israeli government and the bulk of Israeli society were opposed to a massive settlement program in the newly acquired territories and understood that a clear public articulation of their goals, which were deeply religious and mystical, would doom their settlement activities. Their arguments for settlement presented to the government were practical and logical—military needs and legitimate return to historical sites—but the returnees' goals were religious and eventually messianic. Gush Etzion, which began as a place for the return of the displaced residents and their offspring, by the beginning of the twenty-first century had become an area with twenty-two settlements and some seventy thousand residents. [22]

The story of Gush Etzion is particularly instructive because it illustrates the settler political strategy. There was no public acknowledgment of messianic motives. Instead, the settlement leadership presented themselves as the avatars of the early Zionist secular pioneers, whose sacrifice and heroism against all odds paved the way for the creation of the modern state of Israel. Those early socialist Zionists were antireligious but sought to reclaim the land and return to an ancestral homeland. Here too were settlers reclaiming Jewish historical rights to the holy land. However, the land was properly owned and legitimately purchased by Jews in pre-state Palestine. In the view of the returning settlers, and indeed in the view of most Israeli Jews, the Etzion bloc was Jewish land stolen in war and the returnees had a moral right to their ancestral home. In this fashion, the messianic settlers early on were able to make common ground with the secular Israeli establishment. History and ethnic memory matter in state policies, even in the modern societies, and the hold of the sacred and historic places on the Israeli imagination deeply influenced even the most secular diplomats and politicians and animates the entire Zionist narrative. The mobilization of collective memory and the portrayal of settlement as the righting of past Jewish historical trauma gave the settlers a measure of legitimacy even among their ideological and political opposition.

The successful settler strategy in settling the Etzion bloc was used in other settlement ventures. In summary, this strategy was as follows: (1) the settler movement would choose an area for settlement that had important connections to Jewish history and to the biblical accounts of ancient Jewish settlement; (2) a small avant-garde group would seek access to the area in the occupied territories, claiming to visit for a short period for religious or historical purposes; and (3) the pioneering group would refuse to leave, demonstrating and confronting the government and challenging the military and the police who sought to evict them. This civil disobedience, sometimes escalating to violence, would be reinforced by lobbying and political deal making with the help of sympathetic parliamentarians and military officials. If this initial attempt was successful—and it often was—large family groups would be recruited for settlement, and thus without public awareness, these usually illegal settlements would become permanent and official Israeli towns or settlements under Israeli authority and law. The settlers saw this as "creating facts on the ground" that would make any eventual return of these sites to Palestinians difficult if not impossible.

HEBRON: FAITH, SETTLEMENT, AND SACRED HISTORY

This settler strategy was used effectively in the establishment of the Jewish settlement in the historic city of Hebron, located in the Judean hills, an area sacred to Jews but with no military or strategic value. Jewish tradition claims that King David began his glorious reign over ancient Israel in Hebron, and Hebron is the site of the Tomb of the Patriarchs, where the progenitors of the Jewish people, Abraham and Sarah, Isaac and Rebecca, and Jacob and Leah, are buried. Jews have been coming to this site in Hebron for over a thousand years, praying for recovery from illness and believing that from this site a final messianic redemption would come. This is an extraordinary sacred place, a sort of holy of holies in the land of Israel. And for this reason, even under the Ottoman authorities, Jews had attempted to establish settlements in the Hebron area. Most of these attempts were unsuccessful, but by the 1920s Hebron had a small Jewish community and housed the famous Hebron Yeshiva, which attracted rabbinical students from all over the globe. In 1929, Arab extremists attacked the Jewish community, killing dozens of Jews, including American and European yeshiva students. This resulted in the eventual demise of the Jewish community in Hebron. The 1929 massacre, as it became known among Jews, was an event never to be forgotten. Here were Jews living in a holy city peace-fully who were massacred and their survivors forced to leave for no other reason than that they were Jews. The loss of Jewish presence in this holy city was never to be forgotten.[23]

After the 1967 war, Hebron came under Israeli military control, but the Israeli government forbade any Jewish settlement in the city. Young religious Zionists, many of them veterans of the war, understanding the religious and messianic significance of the site and the deep attachment felt even by the largely secular and atheistic government officials, peti-tioned to have a Jewish community established in Hebron. The govern-ment was adamantly opposed. The Hebron Arabs were known for their fierce opposition to Jewish settlement, and unlike the Etzion bloc, Heb-ron was far removed from any surrounding Jewish community and deep into areas of Palestinian residence. The government would not permit settlement, but the young Zionists, organized and financed under the banner of the Gush Emmunim, found a creative solution to the settle-ment prohibition. Under the leadership of the charismatic rabbi Moshe Levinger, a few dozen young Gush Emmunim activists with their fami-lies posing as tourists asked the Israeli military authorities permission to spend the 1968 Passover holidays at a hotel in Hebron, promising to leave after the conclusion of the festival. They never left.

When the holiday was over, the settlers refused to leave and invited other members of the Gush Emmunim movement to join them. Though the settlers were illegal occupants of the city and Jewish settle-ment was expressly forbidden, they organized a yeshiva school on the site and made plans for a permanent settlement. Money for the new enterprise came from wealthy donors from the United States who iden-tified with the settlement plans. Political support for settlement also came from leading Israeli politicians such as Yigal Allon and Moshe Dayan, who though secular and not sharing the religious agenda of the settlers still were deeply moved by their pioneering spirit and willing-ness to sacrifice for the cause of settlement in this sacred biblical area. The settlers were also somewhat supported by the European-born prime minister Levi Eshkol and the legendary founding prime minister Ben-Gurion. These Israeli leaders were ambivalent about the settle-ment enterprise deep in Palestinian territory and the potential violence and hostility it could bring, but the biblical and historical qualities of Hebron and the pioneering spirit and commitment and courage of the young settlers encouraged the Israeli authorities to give tacit permission to a permanent settlement in the Hebron area. A pivotal event for government officials was a bomb attack on religious pilgrims and tourists during a 1968 Sukot holiday excursion to the sacred sites in Hebron in which almost fifty Israelis and foreign tourists were killed. The feeling at the time in governmental circles was that the Israelis had won the war and wanted to make peace, and here are these young committed Zionists, a bit extreme but good Jews and citizens, who were being killed for nationalistic goals. While the official Israeli position was that no permanent settlement should take place in these heavily populated Arab areas, the terrorist attack and the settlers' willingness to die for their cause overcame the initial government objection to settlement in Hebron.[24]

To the local Arab residents and the larger Muslim world, Jewish residence in Hebron, an all-Arab city with a strong religious tradition and a highly traditional Muslim population, was an insult to Muslim sensitivities and an intrusion into Dar al-Islam, lands theologically required to be under sole Muslim sovereignty.[25] The international community also objected to settlement and categorized it a foreign occupation and a clear violation of international law. There was also opposition to Jewish settlement from some important Israeli diplomats and politicians, such as Abba Eban, who was the Israeli ambassador to the United Nations, and important elements in the Israeli military command, who saw the Hebron settlement as exacerbating tensions and leading to ethnic and religious violence. To Rabbi Levinger and his followers in the Gush Emmunim movement, these objections were senseless and immoral. In this view, the international community's objections were based on a historical anti-Semitism and a refusal to allow Jews to return to the full borders of their ancient homeland. The objection of the Israeli governmental officials to permanent settlement was the result of religious faithlessness and the fear and terror of Gentile condemnation brought about by centuries of persecution and pariah status. For these religiously motivated Zionist settlers, the time for compromise and diplomatic niceties was over. The 1967 victory was a divine call, a command, an obligation, a *mitzvah* to settle the historic cities and sacred places all over the Holy Land. This was not foreign occupation but historic return of Jews to ancestral homes.

From its beginnings after the 1967 war with a handful of families ostensibly coming for a holiday outing, the Hebron community has a current population of some five hundred families and with several allied communities a combined population of around ten thousand in the larger Hebron area.[26] The Hebron and Etzion settlements were pivotal events in the settlement enterprise in the West Bank that provided the strategy and tactics of messianic Zionism and served as models for successful settlement expansion throughout the captured territories.

OFRA: RECLAIMING HISTORY

Following the successes in Hebron, the young religious activists in the pioneering Gush Emmunim organization began laying the foundation for establishing a settlement in the northern West Bank, on the main road between Jerusalem and Nablus in an area heavily populated by Palestinians and adjacent to a large Arab town. The choice of this area by the Zionist activists was not coincidental, as the Gush activists wanted to demonstrate the new Israeli sovereignty over the entire Palestinian areas, including the most populated regions. The area chosen for the future settlement was the site of the biblical city of Ofra, which was at one time a Judean capital city and an important settlement of the Hashmonaim clan, the heroes of the Jewish holiday of Hanukah who had triumphed over the Syrian forces in 166 BCE. The left-leaning Labor government at the time was strongly opposed to any Jewish settlement in this volatile area and adamantly refused any permission to establish a Jewish presence there. As in Hebron, the activists found a way around the official prohibition. At first, they simply illegally camped out in tents and trailers and announced that a new settlement had been established. The Israeli military police with strong government backing forcibly removed the militant squatters. They returned several times on various false pretenses and again and again were forcibly evicted.

Finally, with help from Gush activists all over the country and with the cooperation of sympathetic lower-echelon officials, the young activists, as a ploy to have access to the Ofra area, asked to do excavating and construction work for the army and were able to get permission to work in the area with the proviso that they leave each evening and return to Jerusalem. After a time, the young radicals—twenty men and three women—refused to leave in the evening and challenged the military authorities to forcibly remove them, threatening widespread civil disobedience if they were harmed in an eviction attempt. The threat of civil disobedience worked, and a compromise was reached permitting a small group of Gush activists to live on the site. This small group of "workers" never left the so-called construction area. Once the government gave in to their modest "overnight" settlement demands, the workers had several families move to the site, and within a few years dozens of families came and a town was built with schools, small craft shops, synagogues, and eventually a central religious high school for religious girls from all over the country. Until 1977, Ofra was tolerated as an "illegal" settlement but did not have official status as an Israeli community. With the election of the right-wing Likud party in 1977, Ofra was recognized as an official Jewish community, which meant it was entitled to funding for its economic and social and educational institutions. The community greatly expanded under the Likud government and is now a vibrant small town. Some of the most prominent leaders in the messianic Zionist movement now live in Ofra, and in some ways it stands as an ideological center of the movement. At present, with a population of about four thousand people in an area covering several miles, Ofra is a bustling community with lots of families and young children and visiting students attending seminars sponsored by the Yesha movement. A manufacturing plant and a small but distinguished winery also now operate in the community.[27]

OPPOSITION TO THE SETTLEMENTS

The rise and development of the two communities, Ofra and Hebron—now two of over a hundred settlements, cities, towns, and settler outposts all over the West Bank—provided the blueprint for settlements all over the conquered territories as religious Zionists sought to settle the whole land of Israel in accordance with their messianic agenda. It was no easy task to develop and build the settlements. Amid the sense of confidence that was engendered by the 1967 victory, there was still a deep Israeli yearning for peace with their Arab neighbors and a strong desire neither to antagonize the Arab world nor to risk international censure for what the international community had judged to be an illegal and immoral occupation of Palestinian land. The longtime ruling Labor party, the Israeli intellectual and artistic elite, and the military establishment, with very few exceptions, were firmly opposed to the settlement activities in Judea and Samaria. Furthermore, they understood that creating small Jewish enclaves in heavily populated Arab areas would only result in more conflict and tension, with the Israeli state being seen as a colonialist power ruling over a conquered people with no political rights. The secular elites wanted a democratic Jewish state with a clear Jewish majority, and the annexation of lands with over a million Arabs would end their dream of a uniquely Jewish state. For the secular elites, continued occupation and settlement would surely lead to ethnic and religious violence, international condemnation, and the breakdown of a truly democratic, egalitarian Israeli political system. Yitzhak Rabin, the Israeli general and prime minister in the 1970s who was murdered by a zealous messianic Zionist in 1995, early on gave voice to the concern of many Israeli moderates and establishment leaders when he said that he saw the settlement movement "as a very grave phenomenon—a cancer on the body of Israeli democracy."[28] The settlers' messianic talk, their refusal to abide by governmental regulations, their secret closed meetings, their reliance on older charismatic rabbis as their political and religious mentors, and their goal of establishing a Jewish religious theocracy was alien, threatening, and repugnant to Rabin and the secular establishment. Some Zionist rabbis and politicians, including nationalist members of parliament, urged restraint, advising that stronger public support needed to be developed before massive settlement activity was undertaken. The mostly young settler leadership, encouraged by the messianic views of their charismatic mentor, Tzvi Yehuda Kook, demurred. They were not to be stopped; the time had come. The victory was divine and the acquisition of the sacred land in Judea and Samaria was a divine call to settlement. And all those attuned to the call had to act now, swiftly, courageously, faithfully, and with certainty that the divine will be done.[29]

The settlers felt they had a blueprint for success. They had overcome governmental and political obstacles in Hebron and in the Etzion region, and these tactics were used over and over again in establishing towns, villages, and outposts all over the contested territories conquered in the 1967 war. The settlers' approach was always to choose a site that had biblical antecedents—like Hebron—or sites linked with earlier pre-state settlement, as was the case in the Etzion region. The settlers generally asked for a small contingent to settle in the area, arguing that the site had strong Jewish historical significance and that, as victors in the war, Israel should settle the ancestral land. With the exception of settlements around Western Jerusalem, the government was opposed to these settlement attempts and forbade entry to the areas. This resulted in public demonstrations, advertisements in the media, and sophisticated private lobbying with government and military officials, some of whom were quite sympathetic to the settlers and were won over to their position. The argument made in response to governmental opposition, which was almost always the case, was, "This was always Jewish land; we are not taking land from anybody, just reclaiming our historical and Zionist heritage." Moreover, the argument went, in refusing settlement activity, the government was denying its own Zionist past. And even more pointedly, the activists taunted their opposition, "What's the difference between our settling in Hebron or Ofra and your Zionist settlement in the early twentieth century in the Galilee or in expanding the boundaries of the state after the 1948 war? If we are outlaws in settling the West Bank, so were many of our Zionist forebears who were secular, so why single us out as warmongers?"

These disputations continue to this day. I recall going on a bus excursion to visit historic sites in the West Bank with a settlement group leaving from the Binyanei Hauma, the Jerusalem Convention Center, where an international circus was performing. As the mostly secular middle-class ticketholders came by, they could see the small demonstration and the signs held by the settler group urging Jewish settlement and sovereignty in Judea and Samaria. Some of the exhibition visitors were annoyed and challenged the demonstrators, some claiming they were racists in wanting to settle in Palestinian lands. The settlers' supporters fought back, and at one point an elderly man—he appeared to be in his late seventies or eighties—started yelling, "You are all so righteous. Do you know that the convention center where you are going to have a good time was built at the site of the Arab village of Sheikh Badr, which was destroyed by the Israeli Army during the 1947 War for Independence after the local Arab population fled? I know, I was a soldier fighting in Jerusalem during that battle for this site. Stop being hypocritical, acting so high and mighty."

THE CONTEMPORARY SITUATION

The current settler situation in the early decades of the twenty-first century is complex and much in flux. There is still Israeli opposition to the settler movement, but full and fervent opposition is found only among far-left groups, such as the Meretz party and the radical antisettlements group Peace Now. The bulk of Israeli society, including the left-of-center secular parties, has come to terms with the settlements. This does not mean they concur at all with the settler agenda or ideology, but they see at least some of the settlements as permanent and legitimate additions to the Jewish state. Secular Israelis may not like the fundamentalist settler religion, but most concede that some of the settlement towns and villages serve as buffers against an Arab attack. Among the settlers, there are also serious divisions. The current Yesha hard core, which I refer to as "activist messianists," support the construction of illegal settlements all over the West Bank and refuse to follow Israeli legal procedures to obtain government permits to establish new settlements. The activists see themselves as the messianic avant-garde and are willing to challenge the government, police, and army in their goal of settling the whole of Judea and Samaria. The largest group of settlers I term "passive messianists," who are determined to settle the whole biblical Land of Israel but want to do this by political means, lobbying and publicity convincing the larger Israeli populace about the desirability and legitimacy of the settlement enterprise. The two groups often battle each other over tactics, ideology, and willingness to compromise. Nonetheless, they share a common religious Zionist outlook and see the emergence of the state of Israel and the success of the settler movement as a harbinger of messianic transformation. Despite divisions, the settlement movement overall continues to grow. As of 2014, the consensus among Israeli analysts is that are about 150,000 people living in "settlements" in the greater Jerusalem area (i.e., areas under Jordanian, Syrian, or Egyptian control prior to the 1967 war) and about 350,000 living in the West Bank areas known to Israelis as Judea and Samaria.[30]

This considerable development and expansion of settlements shows that after the rejection of the early Gush Emmunim settlement attempts, the settlers were increasingly successful, and their political standing and ideological agenda, while still opposed by the secular elites, gained considerable public understanding, tolerance, and even acceptance. In the next chapter, we discuss how the growing Yesha settlement movement transformed traditional Jewish culture and theology from political caution and religious passivity to a militant religious nationalism, willing to challenge the secular Israeli government and demand that the government resist international pressure to stop settlement expansion. This was no small feat because Jewish theology and culture are determinedly conservative and oppose militant confrontation. The Yesha rabbis and theologians, as we shall see, were successful in transforming religious culture by using traditional texts and Talmudic sources combined with sophisticated political polemics to construct a militant but still traditionalist Jewish religious Zionist nationalism.

2

FROM ZIONISM TO MESSIANIC NATIONALISM

THE HOLY LAND IN RABBINICAL THEOLOGY

The central concern facing Jewish theology and faithfulness for the last two thousand years has been accounting for the homelessness, persecution, and suffering of the Jewish people since the destruction of the Temple in 70 AD and the demise of the Second Jewish Commonwealth. How was it, from the Jewish self-understanding, that God's chosen people, to whom the Lord had given the Torah, his testament of truth for all humankind, would be destined to be a wandering people and a pariah nation? What was it about the Jews from the times of antiquity to the present that caused this religion and people to be reviled, banished, and, as the twentieth century has shown, the victim of mass murder and genocide? How could the "chosenness of Israel" be reconciled with the Jewish historical experience?[1]

The classical rabbinical answer was that nothing had really changed in God's relationship with the Jewish people. They were and remain God's chosen nation, and the Land of Israel remains the Jewish homeland to which all Jews will ultimately return. Exile and homelessness are a passing and temporary phenomenon. They are to be endured because of Israel's sins, because of the Jewish nation's refusal to faithfully observe all of God's *mitzvoth*, commandments, because of their lack of care and love for their brethren, and because of the Jewish tendency to follow alien religions and assimilate to foreign cultures. Israel's exile

from the Holy Land and its difficult diaspora condition are punish-
ments, but, in the Jewish religious understanding, exile is still a sign of
Jewish uniqueness and an essential element in the special covenantal
relationship with God. Jewish homelessness and wandering are terrible
and painful, but they are a necessary atonement for the Jewish return to
the Holy Land, where in due time Jews will again be able to gather at
the Temple, where Jewish worship and cult service will continue. Diaspora, exile, and national suffering will be followed by redemption and
triumph.

The synagogue liturgy captures this Jewish sensibility. "But because
of our sins, we have been exiled from our land and sent far from our
soil. We cannot ascend to appear and to prostrate ourselves before you
and to perform our obligations in the House of your choice, in the great
and holy house in which your name was proclaimed because of the
hand that was dispatched against your sanctuary." There is an admission
of guilt and wrongdoing, but with it a prayer for and faith in a return to
the ancient homeland and to the precincts of the Holy Temple. As the
prayer concludes: "Our father our King reveal the glory of your kingship
speedily upon us, speedily—, Raise us high in the eyes of the multi-
tudes, Draw our scatted brethren from among the nations and bring in
our dispersions from the ends of the earth. Bring us to Zion, your city,
in glad song and to Jerusalem, home of your sanctuary in eternal joy.
There we will perform for you our sacrifices and offerings."[2]

In this view, enshrined in religious texts and folk culture, persecution and homelessness should not be denied but acknowledged as destiny. A Jew's duty is to be patient, accepting and passively awaiting the
future, but certain, apocalyptic, supernatural messianic transformation.
In the meantime, a pious Jew studies the Torah, observes the *mitzvoth*,
and meticulously follows a Halachic family lifestyle, ensuring that future generations be trained in Jewish law and religious culture and
remain faithful to the vision of waiting and future redemption. Engaging in political or military action to restore Jewish sovereignty in the
Holy Land was forbidden and was a sign of religious faithlessness. Jewish wandering and homelessness was a divine decree. This apocalyptic
view of redemption was accepted in Judaism from the time of the
Roman capture of Jerusalem in 70 CE and theologically reinforced
after the failed Bar Kokhba rebellion in 132 CE.[3] Jewish passivity and
statelessness were further supported by a fourth-century discussion in

the authoritative Babylonian Talmud where a Babylonian sage admonished a talented student and colleague for wanting to emigrate from Babylon, the center of diaspora life at that time, to study in a Palestinian yeshiva. The Babylonian's objection was based upon a Midrashic reading of a passage in the Song of Songs known as the "Three Oaths," whereby God vows to protect the Jewish people in the diaspora and eventually bring about messianic redemption if the Jewish people reject any attempt at conquest or seek migration to the Holy Land and do not rebel against or challenge the Gentile nations. The Babylonian sage understood the pious motives of his student but sought to dissuade him from emigration as this was, in the sage's view, a violation of the rabbinical injunction. This Talmud-based passive and apocalyptic messianism became the hallmark of Rabbinic Judaism and continues in contemporary Haredi Judaism. From this point of view, as the historian Jody Myers put it, "God is the actor and the Jews merely supplicants. They are entirely at God's mercy, and the most they can do is plead for attention through their prayers."[4] This passive religiosity appears to have only heightened the yearning for the Jews' return to their ancient homeland. Throughout their diaspora wanderings, the Jews' connection with the Land of Israel remained firm—their eventual return to their sacred homeland was taken for granted—and was constantly affirmed and reaffirmed in liturgy and in the folk culture of song, literature, and popular preaching. All life events and rituals—births, weddings, deaths—concluded with the assurance and certainty of the miraculous messianic transformation and the return to the Holy Land, events not requiring human action or input.

POLITICAL ZIONISM AND JEWISH ACTIVISM

The first political challenge to the dominant rabbinical view was the rise of the Zionist movement in the nineteenth century, which advocated an activist program for the establishment of Jewish settlement in Palestine. Beginning with the writings of iconoclastic Orthodox rabbis like Tzvei Hirsch Kalischer and the rise of the populist "return to Zion" movements in Russia, Lithuania, and Poland, followed by the formal establishment of the political Zionist movement in 1898, these thinkers and movements, both religious and secular, argued for Jewish activism and migration to the Holy Land.[5] Though these movements captured the loyalty of large segments of Jews all over the world, the bulk of Orthodox Jewry and their rabbinical leadership clung to their passive theology and rejected the Zionist movement. To these Orthodox traditionalists, the Zionist movement was heresy and a rebellion against rabbinical authority. It was a secular movement advocating an activist political program in direct violation of the rabbinical injunction for Jews to acknowledge the legitimacy of exile and homelessness and to wait passively for supernatural redemption.[6] Indeed, the modern political Zionist movement was essentially a modern nationalistic and secular enterprise, but it had historical and religious roots. Theodor Herzl, the organizer of the first Zionist congresses and leader of the nascent movement, was a cosmopolitan European journalist and playwright and a highly assimilated Viennese Jew who was far removed from Jewish practice and observance. With few exceptions, the Zionist leadership was secular, socialist, or assimilated. Their goal in their own words was to solve "the Jewish Problem," the inability of Jews to fully integrate and be accepted in European society. In his Zionist manifesto, *The Jewish State*, written in 1896, Herzl explained the dire situation of the Jews in European society:

> No one can deny the gravity of the Jewish situation. Wherever they live in appreciable number, Jews are persecuted in greater or lesser measure. Their equality before the law, granted by statute, has become practically a dead letter. They are debarred from filling even moderately high offices in the army, or in any public or private institution. . . . The fact of the matter is, everything tends to one and the same conclusion, which is expressed in the classic Berlin cry: *Juden raus*, out with the Jews. . . . Shouldn't we get out at once?[7]

There are no clearly articulated religious or messianic themes in this political European Zionism. The bulk of the leaders and thinkers of political Zionism were nonbelievers, more influenced by the flowering of European nationalism than the Bible. The early Zionist program was not concerned with biblical promises or messianic transformation but with practical goals to alleviate marginalization and discrimination against European Jews. In the Zionist narrative, Zionism sought to provide "a land without people for a nation without a land." While this was not the case—there were other peoples living in Palestine—the desire for territory as a Jewish refuge was real and was the clear goal of the movement. The Zionists saw land and a sovereign Jewish state as the solution to Jewish homelessness and persecution, a state where Jews would be liberated from the stigma of racial and religious otherness. The Zionist goal was not a theologically pure Jewish state with distinct Jewish religious laws, values, and observance, but a state where Jews would be finally free of prejudice, discrimination, and the psychological insecurities and trauma that resulted from minority status. The Jewish state would be the place where the Jewish people would be at home, free to be fully human and with opportunities to express the fullness of their human creativity. The ideal state as spelled out in the early Zionist literature was to be a sophisticated modern European democratic republic with universities, art and music, modern industry, and even the use of European languages. The goal was to create a new Jewish nation that would be an equal partner in the international arena and raise the standing and status of Jews all over the world. The "new Jew" in his homeland would erase the stereotypical image of the European Jew. The Jews in the Jewish commonwealth would be physically strong, "muscular," as one Zionist spokesman put it, confident, unafraid, with none of the fears and insecurities of his diaspora forebears.

RABBINICAL OPPOSITION TO ZIONISM

The founders of political Zionism were not so much opposed to religion as they thought it irrelevant and residual.[8] Herzl wrote that there would be synagogues in the new state for those who wanted these institutions, but the rabbis and religious leaders would have to know their limited place in a modern progressive society. The traditionalist rabbinical leadership and most Orthodox Jews were opposed and frequently in deep conflict with the secular Zionist agenda. For these traditionalists, the Zionist leaders were not truly Jewish nor representative of authentic Judaism. They were not observant Jews, and their program was a violation of faithful Jewish waiting for messianic transformation. To the traditionalists, the Zionist movement was the work of the devil as it substituted political action for religious observance, encouraged emigration to Palestine instead of Talmudic study and pious observance, and, worst of all, claimed that human activity instead of divine action would usher in the return to the Land of Israel. Perhaps most disturbing of all, Zionism appealed to many Orthodox young people, who were much attracted to the activist modernity of political Zionism and were now in active rebellion against the rabbinically sanctioned passive messianism. The late nineteenth century and early twentieth century saw massive exodus from traditional Judaism to all sorts of strands of political Zionism. In the view of some traditional European rabbis, Zionism was equated with apostasy and anti-Semitism. So great was the rabbinical opposition to Zionism that even after the German roundup of European Jews in ghettos and the mass extermination of Jews during World War II, some rabbis actively discouraged migration to the "heretical" Zionist environs of Palestine. As the renowned Haredi rabbi and yeshiva dean Elchonon Wasserman put it, "Anti-Semites want to kill the body but Zionists kill the soul. Better to die than consort with the Zionists."[9]

This bitter anti-Zionist animus continues to this day among many Haredi Jews. Even after the establishment of the state of Israel in 1948, there was no recognition of the state as a Jewish commonwealth. Haredi Jews still do not participate in any state holidays, nor will they stand or participate in the singing of the national anthem during state occasions or serve in the Israeli armed forces. The Jewish state, in this view, is an aberration to be lived with but an entity that has no Jewish religious significance. Moreover, it is spiritually contaminating as it seeks to replace pure faith with human action in pursuit of realizing Jewish destiny. The emphasis on political activism and the image of the Zionist Jew as self-reliant, activist, and independent is anathema to the ultra-Orthodox Haredim. The Zionist belief that political statehood and Israeli military power can protect Jews is a dangerous and heretical notion. When the slogan popularized by the radical nationalist Rabbi Meir Kahane, "Never again a holocaust," became popular in Jewish circles, Rabbi Elya Svei, one of the leading rabbis in the American Haredi Agudath Israel organization, declared at a mass rally that those claiming that Jewish activism or military might would deter violence against Jews compromised Jewish faith. "Never again," he declared, was an antireligious, anti-Jewish slogan. "If God wants to bring a Holocaust He will bring it. . . . We can tell God nothing." In this speech, Svei was championing the traditional rabbinic view of passivity and fatalism against which Zionism rebelled.[10]

MIZRACHI: A SYNTHESIS OF RELIGION AND ZIONISM

There was one group of traditionally religious Jews who did not acquiesce to the anti-Zionist position. This group, known as the Mizrachi movement, while a distinct minority in the early Zionist movement, did see Zionism as a valuable and legitimate Jewish movement. Mizrachi followers, and among them were scholarly and distinguished Talmudists, were fully observant and Orthodox Jews, but they acknowledged human agency in the messianic process. They argued that despite the secularism and rejection of traditional Judaism of the Zionist leadership, the movement had great value. The Zionist movement would alleviate Jewish persecution and help develop Palestine as a place of refuge for the persecuted Jewish masses of European society where Jews could ultimately establish a commonwealth based upon religious principles. Their governing slogan was "Torah v' Avodah" (Torah and Labor), and their program called for the establishment of a Jewish state dedicated to biblical truth and to Jewish farming and labor to develop Palestine as a self-sufficient society welcoming all Jews. In this way, they hoped to prepare for the ingathering of the Jewish people to their homeland. In important ways, the Mizrachi were Orthodox rebels who refused to conform to the apocalyptic messianism of the rabbinical establishment and were the ideological forerunners of the Yesha movement. The early Yesha settler leadership was educated in Mizrachi schools and yeshivoth, and they were loyal children of the movement who gave religious Zionism a militant and political outlook.

The Mizrachi, in the pre-state Zionist movement, however, always took a back seat to the secularists who were the Zionist establishment and made the critical political decisions. The Mizrachi leaders cooperated with the secular Zionists, but their goals were different. They did see the creation of a Zionist state as a religious event, but their religious Zionism was muted, limited to liturgy, religious ritual, and holiday celebration, and they did not pursue a political and ideological program. These religious Zionists saw themselves mainly as ensuring a place for religion and ritual observance in the new state, but they did not seek to impose their ideology or demand acceptance of their religious and theological goals. After the state of Israel was established, the Mizrachi movement became a political party and joined every Israeli coalition government until the 1967 war, serving with the leftist, social-democratic Labor party, Mapai. This was the party of the secular Zionist pioneers and of the charismatic first prime minister of Israel, David Ben-Gurion, who had negotiated the partition agreement that ceded parts of the biblical Land of Israel to a future Palestinian state. The Mizrachi party, though religiously committed to Jewish sovereignty over the whole of biblical Israel, still acceded to the agreement and never challenged the foreign policy or domestic agenda of the ruling Mapai party. In exchange for their coalition votes and cooperation, the Mizrachi party and their rabbinical establishment were given the right to function as a kind of religious ritual police. They were successful in ensuring that the Israeli Army and all government institutions would serve only kosher food at official functions—something unnecessary to most Israelis. They were able to obtain government laws maintaining a high level of public Sabbath observance, and they were also able to establish rabbinical authority over marriage, divorce, and the Jewish status of prospective immigrants.

Religious Zionists in the early years of the state were a marginal phenomenon in Israeli society, a tolerated group welcomed for their willingness to be part of the government but never challenging the political or religious status quo. The Mizrachi leadership was open to compromise and with few exceptions did not demand to transform Israel society in conformity with their theological outlook. They clearly had a religious, even messianic, vision—seeing the new state as the "first flowering of redemption," as their new liturgy put it—but their messianic rhetoric did not demand political or military action. They were willing to wait, and they were in retrospect quite evolutionary and patient. They never demanded territorial expansion and were circumspect in their religious demands. Their rabbis generally avoided politics and the public domain and saw their roles as being in the religious and educational realms. Religious Zionism until after the 1967 war was burdened with a sense of inferiority, even shame. The state of Israel and the preceding Aliyah movements and pioneers who built the pre-state foundations, and the Zionist movement itself, which provided the political leadership, were secular and in large measure antireligious. Religious Zionists knew that the Mizrachi movement was a latecomer and a distinct minority of the Zionist movement, and it was best for them not to press their religious and quasi-messianic agenda on what they understood was a largely secular Israeli culture.[11]

THE 1967 WAR: RELIGION AND POLITICS TRANSFORMED

The success of the 1967 war, which transformed Israeli society, had its greatest impact on the religious Zionist community, particularly the young religious Zionist yeshiva students who fought in the war, some quite heroically.[12] Most of these young veterans had grown up in religious Zionist Mizrachi schools and communities, and their religious vision for the state had never been realized. They were Israelis, but their lifestyle, beliefs, and political and religious goals were far removed from the Israeli populace and the Israeli government. They and their religious Zionist parents loved the Jewish state, but they were accepted as authentic and legitimate by neither the religious Haredim, who saw them as compromising tradition, nor the Israeli establishment, who similarly saw their religiosity and Orthodoxy as medieval, benighted, and threatening to their goals for a modern state. For those religious Zionists who would go on to form the Gush Emmunim messianic settlement movement, the 1967 victory was proof that the religious Zionist agenda with its full messianic goals was correct and was now to be implemented without embarrassment or inferiority. To these yeshiva-trained and -empowered religious Zionists, the victory had transformed Jewish destiny and was a clear indication that the messianic process had truly begun. What till now was prayerful liturgy and faithful yearning was reality. Jerusalem was reunited as a Jewish city for the first time in two thousand years; the West Bank areas of Judea and Samaria, the sites of ancient Jewish settlement and the places where the Patriarchs had lived, were now under Israeli sovereignty. This was then, to the young religious Zionists, no ordinary military event but God's intervention on behalf of his beleaguered people and God's call to his faithful to pursue Messianic transformation. Here was evidence that Jewish power and military action could transform Jewish destiny. Mere passive waiting for redemption, the traditional yearning for an apocalyptic end to homelessness and exile and the Jewish aversion to political and military power had to end. God had now called his people to pursue their nationalist and religious destiny.[13]

This young generation of religious radical Zionists did not share their parents' sense of inferiority as second-class Zionists—they were mostly native born and army veterans—nor did they feel less religious than the non-Zionist Haredim or insecure in their Talmudic and rabbinical training. Many leaders of the new radicals, such as Hanan Porat and Moshe Levinger, were ordained rabbis and talented Talmudists who had studied in elite yeshivoth and were lifelong students of the legendary Rabbi Tzvi Yehuda Kook. They saw their own scholarship and religious practice as exemplary and the equal of the traditional Haredi Orthodox. They were, similarly, not to be deterred by the largely secular Israeli establishment, who were openly hostile to their messianic agenda and even more so to their militant politics and settlement agenda. These post-1967 religious nationalists were in rebellion against secular Zionism as well as Haredi religiosity and their own parents' generation, with its quiescent, noncombative religious Zionism. They wanted to be and indeed did become militant religionists and nationalists, a type that had not existed in Judaism for millennia.[14] To these new religious nationalists, the state was a sacred religious phenomenon, the army was a religious entity, and the politics of settlement was a religious path for messianic transformation. Zion was not merely a safe haven, a place of escape for persecuted Jews, or just another nation whose people happened to be mostly Jewish; it was a vehicle for world transformation. The 1967 victory was a divine call for Israel to complete the process of messianic transformation predicted in sacred scripture and much longed for in Jewish history. Much was in place, but the fullness of Jewish sovereignty over Eretz Yisrael was yet to be realized. Territorial expansion and settlement over the entire biblical Land of Israel became the central task of the new religious nationalists, and the settlement process began. In the years after the 1967 war and the Yom Kippur War of 1973, several settlements were established by religious nationalists in the acquired territories. The settlement enterprise really got under way after the 1973 Yom Kippur War with the establishment of the then umbrella settler organization Gush Emmunim, which ideologically, politically, and financially was the prime organizational base for the settlement movement and was much influenced by the religious nationalism teachings of the charismatic Rabbi Tzvi Yehuda Kook.

THE 1973 YOM KIPPUR WAR

The Yom Kippur War of 1973, coming just six years after the Six-Day War and in which Israeli forces were hit by a surprise attack that resulted in the loss of thousands of lives, shook Israel's confidence and deeply muted the optimism and expansionism of Israeli society. The religious nationalist students of Rabbi Kook and their followers, however, preached that the war losses were a further test for Israel, that not enough was being done to advance the messianic process, and that Jews were delinquent in not aggressively establishing settlements over the whole of the Land of Israel. Following the 1973 war, this group formally established Gush Emmunim, the Bloc of the True Believers, which took as its central and essential task to settle the whole land of Israel. The Gush settler movement paid respect to the contributions of secular Zionism but believed that the Israeli government and society had become too Westernized and had substituted ordinary secular nationalism for the religious messianic nationalism demanded of the Jewish people. They, the Gush Emmunim settlers, were the true Zionists; they were unafraid of the "Goyim," the nations of the world, and unlike the complacent Israeli establishment were willing to stand up to the world in order to bring full sovereignty in the Land of Israel. The Gush as an organization operated for many years with much success and despite serious internal disputes over ideology and tactics was successful in establishing key settlements in the new territories. Gush Emmunim was later followed by the Yesha organization, which became the umbrella organization for the settlement communities. The settler movement, however, as we shall see, is complex and has many ideological and political factions, but all share a common view of the legitimacy of Israeli settlement and Jewish sovereignty over the whole Land of Israel.

ZIONISM, SETTLEMENTS, AND THE MESSIANIC ERA

The theological basis of the settler movement lies in their view that the conditions for messianic redemption have begun in the contemporary state of Israel. This means that Judaism and Jewish identity must be transformed. The earlier traditionalism eschewing political activism and national Jewish rights must be rejected. The divine call, in the religious Zionist view, is for Jews now to establish sovereignty and to settle the whole of the Land of Israel. It is this religious worldview that motivates and legitimates the expansionist settlement program and the group's radical nationalist politics.

Settlers do not see their theology or politics as a rejection of Jewish traditionalism but as an affirmation and execution of traditional rabbinical doctrines calling for the eventual return to the Land of Israel in fulfillment of God's covenantal relationship with the Jewish people. The settlers proudly proclaim that biblical promises made to the Jews as God's chosen people entitle them to eternal sovereignty in the Land of Israel and that in messianic times all Jews will return to their Holy Land, where they will establish a harmonious society that will serve as an inspirational "light unto the nations" and bring peace and tranquility to the entire world. This view of Jewish chosenness and eternal return are central to traditional Jewish theology, and there is no dissent on these issues. The notion of Jewish settlement and the religious duty of all Jews to make their home in the Land of Israel, and even to engage in religiously sanctioned war to reclaim and protect Jewish interests in the Land of Israel, are all ideas and Halachic guidelines inscribed in traditionalist texts and in canonical law.[15] In maintaining this theological position, the Yesha settler religious theology is fully consonant with Jewish biblical and rabbinical teachings. The great novelty of the Yesha movement is that it has implemented these traditionalist religious beliefs and rabbinical directives, long thought to be practically irrelevant, into a viable and ongoing political program. Put differently, Yesha faith and theology are normative and traditional; what is new and radical is the religious will and sanction to implement these old theological truths.

Yesha theologians argue that this is precisely the religious significance of the modern state of Israel. The old texts can be brought to life, implemented by faithful Jews who are religiously willing to recognize the radically changed conditions of Jewish life. Mass *Aliyah* (Return) to the Holy Land now is not a dream; living in Hebron or the old city of Jerusalem and praying at the Tomb of the Patriarchs, or settling in Kedumim, adjacent to the site of the biblical city of Shechem, is not a fantasy but a daily reality as courageous Jewish settlers act to take back their sacred land. The passivity and fearfulness associated with diaspora life must be rejected, and Jews must be willing to engage in war and battles as ancient Jewish warriors did, encouraged by religious texts that have been ignored for millennia. The settlers did not create the expansionist theology but gave it life, transforming religious longing into practical politics. These nationalistic policies and goals appear radical, but they are grounded in traditional rabbinical and Talmudic texts and articulated by scholars recognized as bona fide authorities in the world of traditional Jewish literature and jurisprudence. Moreover, the style of theological thinking, the mode of reasoning, and the textual justification for messianic Zionists is based upon authoritative traditional theological texts and authorities acknowledged by all sectors of Orthodox Judaism, including the anti-Zionist Haredim. The Haredi rabbis disagree, argue, claim that the Zionist scholars are misinterpreting sources—but they cannot deny the legitimacy and accuracy of the textual sources or that disagreements, if faithful to the textual sources, are the norm in Halachic disputation and *psak*, decision making. Furthermore, the proponents of the new nationalistic religious Zionism, while creating a novel synthesis of Orthodoxy and activist nationalism, were firmly observant and traditional in their Jewish lifestyle. While the earlier Mizrachi religious Zionists were Orthodox, many of their institutions did not follow strict ritual observance and modesty rules, and this lessened their religious standing in the traditional community. The post-1967 generation, particularly its rabbinical leadership, is extremely meticulous in ritual observance, dress, and kosher diet and, with the exception of their religious nationalist agenda, shares much of the religious culture of Israeli Haredim.[16]

MESSIANIC THEOLOGY: THE INGATHERING OF JEWS IN THE LAND OF ISRAEL

The worldwide Jewish migration to the Land of Israel is another distinctive indication of the fulfillment of messianic prophecy. In the settler worldview, evidence that the messianic process has begun is seen in the growing return of Jews to the Land of Israel in a process known in the rabbinical canon as the "Ingathering of the Exiles." Millions of Jews hitherto scattered all over the globe have immigrated to the state of Israel—sometimes en masse—including from Middle Eastern countries like Egypt, Morocco, Yemen, Syria, and Iran. Less massive but also significant are the migrations from Europe and the United States, from Africa and South America, as well as from India. Here is empirical evidence, say the Yesha faithful, that the messianic process is ongoing.

In the words of an authoritative movement rabbi, Yaakov Moshe Bergman:

> Thus we can definitively say that the redemption has begun to unfold before our very eyes. These are not just *signs* of the imminent redemption; they are the beginnings of redemption itself. The pioneers who returned to the Land in large numbers, building and preparing for the return of millions more Jews, precipitated the redemptive process through their actions. After centuries of desolation, the land bore its fruit once again. Five million Jews [now in 2014 over six million] have assembled in *Eretz Yisrael* (literally, the Land Israel) and the ingathering has begun.[17]

The theological significance of a mass return to the Land of Israel as a messianic event is not to be minimized. Talk of the Jewish return at the end of time was always identified with messianic transformation, and it is not at all a novel Jewish theological notion nor unique to the religious Zionist settler movements. Notions of a mass return of the world's dispersed Jews as a prelude to messianic redemption are based upon biblical prophecies and are codified in Talmudic and medieval literature and in the authoritative Maimonidean *Mishnah Torah* and the binding legal text *Shulchan Aruch*, both of which serve as governing rules for Orthodox Jewish belief and practice. Nahmanides, another major medieval legal authority whose positions are still considered binding by many, is perhaps the most explicit among the medieval commentators in seeing the ingathering of Jews as the beginning of messianic redemption.

> The beginnings of the future redemption will occur with the permission of kings. Some of the exiles will gather in Eretz Yisrael and afterward, Hashem will extend His hand again. The verse therefore tells us "The Lord your God will bring you back from your captivity and have mercy on you, and He will gather you together from among the nations to which He scattered you." . . . Hashem, Your God will bring you to the Land that your forefathers possessed and you shall possess it; He will do good to you and make you more numerous than your forefathers.[18]

This view was already discussed in the Babylonian Talmud and in rabbinical literature throughout the ages. The late-twentieth-century rabbinic sage Rabbi Eliezer Waldenberg, famed for his Halachic work *Tzitz Eliezer*, captured the rabbinical consensus when he wrote, "The very gathering of Jews in Eretz Yisrael is a tell tale sign of the beginnings of redemption"[19]

These biblical and rabbinical texts have animated Jewish theology and religious culture for the last two thousand years of exile and dispersion and have maintained Jewish faith and certainty in an eventual release and relief from homelessness and insecurity. The non-Zionist Orthodox Haredim do not deny the reality of the contemporary ingathering but refuse to acknowledge any messianic dimension to the current mass migration to Israel. For them, all the facets of messianic transformation will come in one apocalyptic moment though supernatural and divine action. Anything other than passive waiting is a sign of faithlessness and heresy and bespeaks substituting human agency for divine intercession. To the Zionist settler rabbis, messianic transformation comes in stages and through human activity and political will. There is a divine agenda, but faithful and courageous Jews must do their part in carrying out the divine plan. Rabbi Tzvi Yehuda Kook, the charismatic founder of the movement, put it plainly: "The revelation of the redemption comes through the ingathering of the exiles, and not through miracles."[20] This is really the defining line for the messianic Zionist theology. The messiah is not a onetime event based upon faith alone but a human task for which faithful Jews must dedicate themselves if the divine promises are to be realized. Settlement and reclaiming the whole of the biblical Land of Israel is a religious duty, a sacred task, an obligation of the faithful in their quest to usher in messianic redemption.

THE REJUVENATION OF THE HOLY LAND

The second stage in the messianic process is the rejuvenation and rebuilding of the Land of Israel. Here again Yesha believers can point, in their understanding, to the fulfillment of biblical promise. The astounding successes of Israeli agricultural production, from a land virtually a desert for thousands of years with inhabitants living in near starvation to a land with the most successful agricultural and farm production in the world, is proof that the messianic process is unfolding. Similarly, Israeli successes in medicine, technology, and academia are, to religious Zionists, empirical proof that the biblical prophecies of messianic redemption are occurring for all to see.[21] In the religious Zionist view, only the mass Jewish return to the land of Israel makes this possible. No other nation, religion, or ethnic group could be successful in rejuvenating the desolate Land of Israel. For religious Zionist believers, the failure of all others to develop the land throughout history and the contemporary successes of the Zionists are proof that the Jews are the true inheritors of the land as foretold in the Jewish biblical and rabbinical literature.[22]

In the settler understanding, Israeli successes are clear signs of divine blessings and the special providence promised to the Jewish people upon their return to the Holy Land. This view of Jewish uniqueness and its special connection with the Land of Israel is not a new theological creation but an essential part of the classical rabbinical tradition. The Hebrew Bible talks about the inhospitality of the Land of Israel for foreigners, and the great rabbinical authority Maimonides explained that ever since the Jews were forced to leave the Holy Land, "it has not accepted any other nations: and they all try to settle it, but are unsuccessful." Rabbinical writings all follow this approach, seeing a sacred, even mysterious, connection between Jews and the physical Land of Israel.[23] This religious view of Israeli successes and the legitimacy and impetus it gives to settlement and territorial expansion is unfathomable to those outside the settler community. To the settlers, they are engaged in a divine–human enterprise that will result in the fulfillment of God's plan for the universe. The events now occurring in the modern state of Israel are to them the realization of biblical promises, while in the view of the world community and even to most secular Jews, this is the result of entrepreneurial prowess and political acumen.

RELIGION, SOVEREIGNTY, AND HOLY WAR

The ingathering and the blessings that flow are wondrous, but the messianic process must continue with full Jewish settlement and sole sovereignty over the whole of the land of biblical Israel, Eretz Yisrael. If the messianic process is to reach its full potential, it is faithful Jewish believers, true Zionists, who by their dedication and sacrifice will establish national Jewish sovereignty. Here is why settlement, land, and sovereignty are so critical to Yesha. It is the theological sine qua non for messianic redemption. The settlers are correct in claiming that the goal of establishing Jewish sovereignty over the whole of the Land of Israel is enshrined in Jewish theological, Talmudic, and Halachic texts as a prelude to the fulfillment of Jewish destiny. In this they are following classical rabbinical teachings that the messianic era will only come about through full Jewish settlement and a Jewish state. Their theological activism, nonetheless, leads to grave political and military conflict. What happens if there are other peoples and nations who oppose this Jewish demand for settlement and sovereignty? What happens if there other residents who claim the land as well? Here Jewish theology demands holy war. The messianic process that requires Jewish settlement and sovereignty justifies and obligates waging war against those who oppose Jewish destiny. Tzvi Yehuda Kook, following the positions of several medieval authorities, including both Maimonides and Nahmanides, explains that "although war isn't a desirable or pleasant thing, it is forced upon us by the realities of establishing a state." Moreover, Kook argues, "the Torah commands us to have a state, and if there is a need for conquest and war to fulfill this, then we are compelled to do so. This is one of the 613 precepts of the torah."[24]

This means that there is rabbinical approval for holy war to establish Jewish sovereignty in the Land of Israel. The accusation from settler opponents, both religious and secular, that the settlers have no religious credibility or theological legitimacy for holy war is entirely incorrect. In the Yesha reading, the rabbinical consensus throughout the Talmudic, medieval, and modern periods is that Jewish sovereignty, political authority, and holy war for the Land of Israel are a mitzvah obligation for the Jewish people throughout the ages. True, there were rabbis who objected to massive Jewish settlement and holy war, but these older objections to Jewish settlement and sovereignty were based on Jewish dispersion and statelessness. Now with the state of Israel established and the ingathering of the Jewish people and the messianic process well on their way, Jewish settlement and sovereignty over the full Land of Israel must take place. One of the leading American Talmudists and a former professor of Talmud at Yeshiva University, Rabbi Aron Soloveitchik, justified holy war on this basis. Soloveitchik maintained that waging war to defend the territorial integrity of the Land of Israel in situations of threats to full Jewish sovereignty obligates the Jewish nation to engage in war to defend Jewish rights over the whole Land of

Israel.[25] This means that older discarded doctrines of biblical holy war—*Milchemet Mitzvah*—have now become relevant in the struggle to establish Jewish sovereignty over the Land of Israel. Consequently, as Rabbi Aron Soloveitchik explained, "it is obligatory for the Jewish people to engage in battle"[26] against any Gentile nation that seeks to deter Jews from establishing rights to the whole of the Land of Israel. Soloveitchik and others acknowledge that passivity and avoidance of war were the Jewish norm, but this was because of Jewish weakness and political and military impotence. In the changed conditions of an independent and militarily strong Jewish state, religious justifications for war are now legitimate and desirable.

The settler insistence on Jewish control and sovereignty over the whole Land of Israel is at the core of settler theology and politics. In this, many, though not all, Yesha settlers remain loyal to their charismatic founder, Tzvi Yehuda Kook, who when asked about territorial compromise for peace, explained, "There is absolutely no room to entertain thoughts of relinquishing even a single square meter of Hashem's inheritance to us. There is not to be any blemish in our borders, G-d forbid. We are to battle for this to the end without any surrender."[27] The integrity of the full Land of Israel remains a core settler belief, but given international pressure some moderate settler rabbis acknowledge that territorial compromise is possible, though all privately and most publicly demand full Jewish control and sovereignty. In their insistence on settling all the Land of Israel, the settlers are often viewed as having created a land-based ideology seeking to rule over the local population for purely fanatical religious reasons. The fact of the matter is that the goal of important elements of both pre-state secular Zionism and religious Zionism was precisely to establish a Jewish state on both sides of the Jordan River, including the areas now referred to as the West Bank. The pre-state Zionist right-wing Revisionist party headed by Vladimir Zeev Jabotinsky, which later became the nationalist Herut party headed by Menachem Begin, opposed the partition plan to create two states and insisted, unsuccessfully, on including all areas of biblical Israel in the newly established 1948 Jewish state. There is, therefore, both much religious basis and cultural memory for settlement in Judea and Samaria. In their insistence on Jewish sovereignty, the Yesha movement continues core classical Zionist ideology and politics that give their settlement program historical legitimacy and still evoke sympathy even among some of their detractors.[28]

MESSIANIC ZIONISM AND THE TRANSFORMATION OF JEWISH IDENTITY

For the settler movement and their religious Zionist followers, this new messianic condition must transform Jewish religion, culture, and psychology. Jews and Judaism must be liberated from a sense of home-lessness and inferiority. The return of the Jews to their ancient home-land and the establishment of Jewish sovereignty in the Holy Land dictate that Israeli Jews reject their view of themselves as a weak, pas-sive, and submissive people, so deeply embedded in the Jewish psyche. Jews and Jewish leaders must refuse to be intimidated by international pressure and actively pursue a policy of territorial expansion whereby all the biblical lands promised to the ancient Israelites in the biblical narratives come under Israeli jurisdiction. In the settler view, messianic times call for aggressive occupation, fearlessness, and risk taking. What is necessary is for Jews to outrightly assert their historical and religious rights to all of biblical Israel. The West Bank territories taken in the 1967 war cannot be surrendered and must remain under Israeli juris-diction and Jewish sovereignty. Here we see the confluence of religion, radical politics, and psychological transformation. The settler's position is that the "miracles" and successes associated with the state of Israel cannot remain a matter of religious fervor and thanksgiving alone but must result in political, theological, and psychological transformation.[29]

Along with this messianic ardor has come an assertion of the impor-tance of Jewish power, confrontation, and risk taking, both with the local Palestinians and with the international community. This new view has resulted in public displays of Israeli authority and power whereby parades and demonstrations are made by settler groups in heavily popu-lated Arab areas, in frequent confrontations between militant settlers and local Arabs, and even in increasing settler confrontations with the Israeli military and police, whom some radical settlers view as weak minded and willing to stop Jewish settlement. These so-called price tag attacks are explained by militant settlers as a means of demonstrating Jewish willingness to defend themselves from terrorist attacks and to show the Palestinian attackers and the Israeli government that any attack on Jewish settlers, including stone throwing, arson, shooting, or personal attacks—all of which are daily occurrences in Judea and Samaria—will be answered with a counterattack. "Price tag" demonstrations, attacks, and violence are also used against the Israeli government by militant settlers in situations when illegal outposts are demolished or when settler groups believe that the government is being passive in the face of attacks on settler property or persons. This is not defended by the official settler leadership, but surveys show that religious Zionists generally approve of these tactics.[30]

The settlers are aware of the unpopularity of their settlement activities and ideology among secular Israelis and of the international repudiation of continued Israeli sovereignty and settlement in the West Bank areas. The dangers of continued occupation are real: economic sanctions on Israeli exports, academic boycotts, and international isolation. The settlers view this international response as a rejection of Jewish rights to the Holy Land and as a continuation of historical anti-Semitism. Antisettlement Israelis consider the settlements an impediment to a peace agreement between Palestinians and Israel and see continued settlement in the West Bank as encouraging violence against Israel. In the settler worldview, this violence and international rejection are irrational and ultimately unrelated to settlements, but are expressions of the refusal of the international community to acknowledge the Jewish right to the Land of Israel, fueled by historical anti-Semitism.

Rabbi Zalman Melamed, the senior rabbi of the Bet El settlement in Samaria, answered critics who claimed that the West Bank settlements caused the Palestinian intifada uprisings and international terrorism against Jewish communities, explaining that there were terror attacks against Israeli targets well before the West Bank settlements existed. Melamed spoke for many in the settlement community in linking the often-rabid enmity to settlements to the history of hatred toward Jews. In his view and in the view of most settlers, it is anti-Semitic hatred of the Jews and an attempt to malign the Jewish state that is the basis of opposition to Jewish settlements. This hatred, persecution, and violence against Jews has no rational basis and existed for thousands of years and certainly long before the state of Israel and the emergence of settlements. Hatred of Jews and the Jewish state, in this view, is a divine mystery, not given to human understanding, and so will continue till the full messianic redemption. The misguided and dangerous error of those who oppose settlement is their misunderstanding of the nature and process of Jewish history. Hatred of Jews is endemic, but secular Israelis and secular Jews have become so highly secularized and Westernized that they refuse to recognize the nonrational nature of anti-Semitism.[31] In the settler view, the psychic trauma of Jewish exile and homelessness is so severe that fears of Gentiles, passivity in the face of attack, and a lack of pride and national honor "became instinctual" and embedded in Jewish culture. Throughout centuries of persecution, Jews lost their honor and adapted out of necessity, fear, and anxiety to national passivity and inferiority. The reality of the state of Israel and the dawning of the messianic era demand that Jews no longer bow to any foreign power but assert their national and religious rights.

CONTINUING ANXIETY: THE PRECARIOUSNESS OF THE JEWISH CONDITION

Still, the history and collective memory of persecution and homelessness does not disappear. Concomitant with their ideology of Jewish power and fearlessness is the settler acknowledgment that anti-Semitism is real, continuing, and dangerous. Jews and Judaism, and by extension the existence of the state of Israel, are in perpetual and immediate danger of persecution and annihilation. Things may look promising, the Israel economy does well, the defense forces and the intelligence services are respected all over the world, and science and technology continue to be highly innovative and successful. Nonetheless, Jews, now as throughout history, must remain forever vigilant. The enemies of the Jews are legion, and hatred of Jews and Israel remains eternal. For the settlers, as for most traditional Jews, the remarks of the popular former president of Iran, Mahmoud Ahmadinejad, who vowed "to wipe Israel off the map," are not a political ploy or an exaggeration but an immediate danger from a Muslim state with nuclear capability. The UN resolution equating Zionism with racism—since rescinded—was similarly seen as a call for the destruction of the state of Israel. The bombing of a Jewish community center in Buenos Aires that killed dozens of civilians or the many attacks in large European cities against Israeli diplomats and Jewish citizens are viewed as a resurgence of anti-Semitism, making

Jews feel vulnerable and unwelcome. And the Hamas bombings of the summer of 2014, during which thousands of rockets were fired at Israel, are reminders of the continuing threats to the Jewish state and to Jews all over the world.

In the settler view, the fury against Jews and the Jewish state cannot be justified by settlements, territorial expansion, or the existence of Palestinian refugees displaced after the 1948 war. Many groups experienced dispersion and population exchange as the result of war or political realignment without an international campaign to attack the legitimacy of the new territorial arrangements. India and Pakistan may be in conflict, but the legitimacy of both states is not challenged. Germans, Russians, Serbs, Poles, and Hungarians all underwent some degree of population and territorial exchange after World War II, but the legitimacy of these states is not challenged. In the settler view and in much of Israeli public opinion, it is not Israeli settlement in the West Bank that is at the root of the conflict but the rise of a sovereign Jewish state in the ancient Holy Land that challenges deeply rooted religious notions of the Jews as an alien and wandering people who reject the universalist truths of Christianity and Islam. European secularism, too, is opposed to the Zionist notions of Jewish uniqueness and the Jewish attachment to an ancient sacred homeland. As a settler rabbi put it to me, "Rich or poor, educated or ignorant, state or no state, they hate us." In the settler view, there is no possibility of "land for peace" because settlements are not the issue. It is, in their view, the very existence of a Jewish state that is rejected by the Palestinians. As settlers repeat and reiterate constantly, why was there no settlement of the Arab–Israeli conflict prior to the Jewish settlement of the West Bank? The settlers have a ready response: it is the refusal of Muslim states to recognize a Jewish national entity anyplace in what was Arab Palestine. In the settler view, the central theological doctrines of Islam make peace between Israel and its Muslim neighbors impossible.

> The State of Israel constitutes a double problem from their perspective, for it was established on territory conquered by Islam since its foundation (except for a period of approximately 100 years when it was ruled by the Crusaders); and not only this, but the land of Israel is located in the heart of Muslim territory. Therefore, as far as they are concerned, this is the first place they must conquer—either by sword or guile.[32]

In this view, all Palestinians faithful to Orthodox Islam must seek to eliminate and dismantle the Jewish state. Palestinian moderates and radicals may disagree over tactics and short-term agreements, but all have the same goal: "the dismantling of the State of Israel and the conquering of the entire land of Israel."[33] From the settlers' perspective, it is political naïveté and foolhardy political correctness to blame the settlements for the lack of peace. The issue is not occupation or settlement expansion but the very existence of a non-Muslim entity in the center of Dar al-Islam, the Muslim world.

This perception of the age-old conflict became clear to me in January 2006, when I arrived in Israel with a group of professors and peace activists who were attending an interreligious meeting on peace in the Middle East. Some of the participants were from Western countries, but there were also contingents of clerics from India, Pakistan, Africa, and the Middle East wearing traditional garb. This made quite an impression on some of the religious Jews in the arrival terminal, and one, seeing that I was a Hebrew speaker, wanted to know what was going on with this mixed group. I told him this was a group from many religions and countries who were coming together to explore possibilities for Middle East peace. The gentleman looked at me for a while and then said, "It's impossible; there cannot be any peace here until the Messiah comes," and with that he quickly walked away. This may be seen as extreme, but it appears to mirror the settler culture.

This universal hostility to Jews has been a central theme in the history of Judaism. Given the nature of Jewish powerlessness and statelessness in the diaspora, the Jews responded by avoiding conflict and decrying violent responses to oppression and persecution. The Jews were seen and saw themselves as "people of the book," studious, pacificist, and noncombative. The most violent and bellicose biblical passages in the Hebrew Bible were ignored or reinterpreted to deny their clearly violent directives. In the religious Zionist view, this historical passivity and refusal to fight back, make war, or engage in self-defense is foolhardy and dangerous for a sovereign and independent nation under siege by hostile and aggressive neighbors. Shortly after the declaration of the state of Israel, Rabbi Tzvi Yehuda Kook gave voice to this transformation. As a rabbi and a Talmud scholar, he acknowledged that the Jews were people of the book and Torah scholarship is central to Jewish identity, but quoting a Midrashic passage, he demanded that in the situation of statehood the Jews now must embrace "the sword" as well. Military prowess and the willingness to engage in violence to defend Jews and the Jewish state are necessary in the condition of statehood. Kook insisted that Torah study and ritual observance, once the corner-stones of Jewish religiosity, were not sufficient in the new situation: "the people of the book" must also become "people of the sword."[34] Following Kook, religious Zionist rabbis have transformed the Jewish theologi-cal understandings concerning self-defense, war, and violence. In these new theological formulations, war and violent conflict in securing the sovereignty of the Jewish nation are necessary, moral, and fully justified by Halacha.

RELIGIOUS ZIONISM, DEMOCRACY, AND THE STATE OF ISRAEL

In Yesha thinking, democracy as a form of government is respected and acknowledged as the most superior form of political organization, and democratic nations are viewed as acting in an ethical and moral fashion. It is seen as a system protecting the rights of individuals and minority groups. Democracy, however, for all its good qualities, is a human con-struction, worthy and laudable but inappropriate for the unique situa-tion of the state of Israel, which is, after all, the vehicle for messianic transformation. Jews, Judaism, and the Jewish state, in the settler view, have a special relationship with God that demands that they follow the directives and commandments of the Torah. Democracy is fine for oth-er nations, but the messianic mission of Israel, the chosenness of Israel, and its special covenant with God make it necessary that when there is conflict with religious law or the democratic majority, the rules of the Torah must be followed. In this view, democracy compromises itself by seeking consensus, but Torah is absolute truth and cannot be compro-mised. Rabbi Eliezer Melamed explained that religious Zionists have a serious conflict with those who want to isolate religion from politics. Religion and politics are one unit for the Jewish people, and the teach-ings of the Torah apply to foreign and international affairs as much as they do to prayers and religious rituals. Melamed's position is echoed by virtually all settlement rabbis and leaders, who see the Torah and rab-binical laws as the only legitimate legislation in Israeli society. Where religious law clashes with modern democratic value, whether in issues of politics, family, sexuality, or national security, the religious authority must prevail.[35] Benny Katzover, a veteran settler leader and a resident in the Elon Moreh community, put it plainly: "The main role of Israeli democracy is to disappear. Israeli democracy has finished its role, and it must disassemble and give way to Judaism. All leads toward recognition that there is no other way but to place Judaism at the center, above all else, and this is the answer to every situation."[36] At the heart of this opposition to democracy is the view that the state of Israel is a harbinger of full messianic redemption and must be kept unsullied by the political compromises and moral individualism found in modern democratic societies.

This does not mean that settler politicians or rabbis want to immediately establish a theocracy or demand full compliance with Halacha. There exists in the movement what can be called an evolutionary view of popular government and Western notions of democracy. For the time being, given the secularism of important sectors of Israeli society, the full reality of religious law cannot be fully implemented and would further alienate an already hostile secular elite. Consequently, the movement does not at this moment advocate politically for a state governed by religious law. The ruling ethos of the movement and the religious goal, however, is that an Israeli Jewish state must become a fully religious society governed by Halacha in all areas of life. For now, protecting the religious status quo in having an authoritative state Orthodox rabbinate that regulates marriage and divorce, kosher food laws, and Sabbath observance is sufficient. As the messianic process progresses and with an increasing Orthodox population, the entire state apparatus—politics, economics, the military, and international diplomacy—will come under rabbinical control.

RELIGION AND STATE: THE CASE OF THE GAZA DISENGAGEMENT

All these issues regarding democracy and the authority of a democratically elected government came to the fore and led to a serious clash between the settlers and the government during the Gaza disengagement in August 2005. The government, led by Prime Minister Ariel

Sharon, passed a law mandating that all the settlements, industrial parks, and military installations in the Gaza area settled after the 1967 war must be evacuated and returned to the Palestinian Authority, believing—incorrectly as it turned out—that this unilateral disengagement would lead to greater security for Israel and encourage continued peace negotiations. This was, of course, a total denial of the settlement ideology and activity. Here was a situation where the Gaza settlers, often with great hardship, had committed to settling and building thriving communities, believing they were both fulfilling their religious goals and helping maintain Israel's security, and they were now being abandoned by their own government. Here was a democratic government challenging the settlers from fulfilling God's mandate to the Jewish people. The democratically elected government saw things differently. Here, the government argued, was a chance to move the peace process along, and the loss of Gaza settlements was well worth the price.

For the Gaza settlers and their Yesha supporters, abandoning the settlements would uproot hundreds of families, destroy functioning communities, and be a state-sponsored denial of messianic settlement Zionism. The Gaza settlements had a Jewish population of about nine thousand people, many with young children. The communities were located in a beautiful seashore area with many synagogues, schools, rabbinical seminaries, and successful industrial parks. The Gaza settlements were economically successful and pluralistic—the hothouses where exotic plants were cultivated were internationally known—attracting hard-core settler believers and also secular residents, less for ideology and more for the beach and the attractive location. Moreover, this was no illegal encampment, nor were any local Palestinians displaced by the Israeli government when it planned and approved the Gaza settlements. The government was, however, firm: all of the settlements had to be abandoned and the entire Jewish population had to leave. Compensation was to be paid to those residents who would leave voluntarily. Some, a distinct minority, left their homes, but the bulk of the settlers, especially the committed religious Zionists, refused. The Yesha council and the settler groups brought case after case to the courts, arguing that disengagement violated human and property rights and even arguing, ironically, that the new law was illegal and violated democratic procedures. Massive demonstrations were held, and protesters came from all over the country on behalf of the Gaza residents.

All this was to no avail, and the Israeli Army was brought in to evict the settlers after the High Court ruled on the legality of eviction. The settlers pledged to refuse to cooperate and would not recognize the state's authority, seeing disengagement as a violation of biblical and rabbinical law to settle the Land of Israel and never cede biblical land to foreigners. The settlers barricaded themselves in their settlements, and thousands of sympathizes came from all over Israel and even some from overseas to stop the eviction. The residents and the newly arrived protesters made a human chain, keeping the army and police from entering the settlements, and there were some instances of violence. There was to be no cooperation with the forces of disengagement as the government action was against Torah law.[37]

This was no ordinary civil disobedience but, as the settlers saw it, a religious battle defending God's truth. The government had to be opposed in the name of religious law. The settlers and their supporters were God's infantry, fighting for messianic transformation in loyalty to God's directives to the Jewish people. The leading settler rabbinical authority at the time, Rabbi Avraham Shapira, the head of the flagship religious Zionist Merkaz Harav Yeshiva and a former chief rabbi, came out with a rabbinical verdict stating that "According to Torah law, it is completely forbidden to give land in Israel to a non-Jew." Shapira went further in condemning disengagement; he challenged the government and the Israeli army's legitimacy, and his ruling prohibited religious soldiers from following orders to remove settlers from their homes, even if they received a direct command from their superiors. Jewish Israeli civilians were also told to ignore the directive to cooperate with state authorities in evicting the settlers. Shapira went to the heart of the matter when he articulated a central tenet of settler religious Zionism, proclaiming that all matters of the Jewish state are religious and theological and therefore only rabbis and Talmudic "sages are allowed to render such decisions that affect all of Israel." Shapiro directly challenged the government:

> An order to take part in an evacuation of Jews from their homes in order to give over the land to non-Jews is an order that is against our holy Torah and forbidden to fulfill. Every order that is contrary to Jewish law and compels one to violate the words of the Torah has no validity, is forbidden to fulfill and no person has the authority to deliver it.[38]

THE GREAT DISAPPOINTMENT

All the protests, demonstrations, and the rabbinical outcry, and even the sporadic violence, did not stop the disengagement from Gaza. The Army Special Forces came in—most of these troops were secular and not especially sympathetic—and forcibly removed all the residents, left hundreds of families homeless for years, closed the factories and hothouses, and most painful of all to the settlers, demolished all the synagogues and rabbinical seminaries. Gaza became Palestinian territory and remains so to this day. The disengagement was and remains a traumatic event for the settler community and highlights the tension between the modern state and settler messianic Zionism. The very foundation of settler theology and politics was crushed, not by an invading army or international pressured, but by an elected Israeli government. The state, which in settler theology is the vehicle for messianic transformation, had arrested, even halted, the messianic movement. Some rabbis reinterpreted the disengagement as a temporary setback akin to those encountered by the ancient Israelites in their ultimately successful conquest of the land of Canaan. Others saw this as a terrible defeat for their settlement and messianic agenda that must never be repeated. Many younger settler activists came away with the view that the Yesha response to the disengagement was too weak, too passive, and inappropriately focused on civil disobedience. These more radical settlers argue that an aggressive, even violent, defense of settlement is needed, even if this should put the settlers in direct conflict with police and military authorities. Despite the evacuation and the loss of the Gaza settlements, the bulk of the settlers remain loyal and firm in their messianic theology. The disengagement brought out serious tensions and conflicts between messianic religious Zionism and the modern democratic Israeli state, tensions that are still very much present in contemporary Israeli society.

Despite this setback, the Yesha movement has kept the loyalty of its followers and has captured the commitment of many Jews all over the globe, and in this way it has transformed Judaism, Zionism, and the state of Israel. Begun as a small cadre of believers in the messianic potential of the new Jewish state, the Yesha movement has built dozens of communities, schools, and political organizations and has successfully constructed a new religious nationalism anchored in Rabbinical Judaism but aspiring to transform Jewish life as it looks forward to a messianic future. The settlers see themselves as the true defenders of Eretz Yisrael, the Land of Israel, as promised to the Jews by their God and in the Hebrew Bible. They see themselves as God's infantry in their quest to realize the biblical promises. The Palestinians living in the West Bank, the worldwide Muslim community, and the bulk of the international community view the settlers as usurpers of local Palestinian land and Israel itself as illegal occupiers of another people's national home. In the next chapter, we look at community life, culture, and faith in the settlements and how the Yesha movement has constructed an alternative world to justify and legitimate their worldview and militant Zionist culture in the face of worldwide opposition.

3

FAITH, CULTURE, AND COMMUNITY LIFE

THE SETTLERS: AN ISRAELI COGNITIVE MINORITY

Life in the Yesha settlements is different. Yesha settlers are an integral part of contemporary Israel, but they live at the same time in an alternative social and religious world based upon traditionalist Jewish culture, values, and faith. Their social, political, and religious lives are all directed by their sense of mission in being God's messengers and infantry for establishing Jewish sovereignty over the whole Land of Israel. The Hebrew Bible, the Talmudic teachings, and the medieval commentators are not things of the past but are living documents and directives for life and politics in the here and now. God's promises to the ancient Israelites to inherit the Holy Land, to establish a holy society in accordance with divine law, and in this way to realize the divine plan for messianic transformation are not poetic narratives or something consigned to an ancient past but a realistic and immediate program to be realized by the Jewish faithful. This is not something easily accepted or even understood by modern secular Israelis, and certainly not by the international community. The reality of settler society, the veracity of the ancient texts, and the certainty of Jewish destiny are so far removed from modern consciousness that interactions with outsiders are fraught with deep misunderstanding and suspicion.

At first, when I talked to many Israelis, and particularly to academics and elites, I was shocked and confused by their strong response and even anger at the settlers. This was not always just a result of political disagreement, but rather they had a sense, and rightfully so, that the settlers inhabit an alternate reality. I saw this when I visited the Beth El community, one of the most established and well-known settlements and the home of some of the most prominent settler leaders, located in the Judean hills near the Palestinian city of Ramallah. Rabbi Yehuda Borer, a longtime resident and one of the founders of the community, who was born in Germany but had made his way to the United States to escape the Holocaust and as a young man emigrated to the new state of Israel, took me around the settlement and led me to a beautiful lookout from which I could see a vista of the biblical Land of Israel. Borer was enthusiastic as we took in the scenic panorama and immediately began quoting verbatim from Genesis 13:15:

> And behold! God was standing over him, and He said, I am Hashem, God of Abraham, your father and God of Isaac; the ground upon which you are lying, to you will I give it and to your descendants. Your offspring shall be as the dust of the earth, and you shall spread out powerfully westward, eastward, northward and southward: and all the families of the earth shall bless themselves by you and your offspring. [1]

This passage comes from Genesis, which tells the story of the patriarch Jacob, who, while fleeing the wrath of his twin brother Esau, whose birthright he had taken, comes to a place he called Bet El (literally, the House of God) and there receives this special divine revelation and promise that Jacob's descendants will inherit all the land. Looking right at me, Rabbi Borer said, "Now you may understand why we are here. This is our home; this is a Jewish holy place promised to us by God." Borer went on to describe other biblical events and revelations that he explained took place in the very area where we were standing. Looking over the beautiful biblical landscape, which looked like it had been untouched for centuries, Borer pointed right and left, explaining that over there was the place where the prophet Samuel preached, and in another direction was a spot where the patriarch Abraham had a sacrificial altar, and in other directions were still other biblical sites. To Borer, I saw, these biblical events and personalities were as immediate and relevant as today's news.

This was not an isolated event. Every settlement I visited had its own connections with biblical history. The Shiloh community in the northern West Bank is at the site of the first Jewish tabernacle, the precursor to the grand Jerusalem Temple, and residents have set up a replica of the ancient structure and speak of Eli the High Priest as if he were a current resident. In Kedumim, in the northern Samaria region, residents showed me biblical passages that speak of its closeness to the biblical city of Shechem and its importance for the future redemption. In Ma'ala Levona, a sister settlement to Shiloh, residents and I sat around drinking local wine while the winemaker asked me, "Do you know why we planted vineyards just here? It's all set out in the biblical prophetic writings, and we are following the ancient texts." Sitting one afternoon in the striking Samarian Mountains with a group of settlers, one resident expressed his frustration: "Can you imagine, there are politicians, wise people, who want to give up and have us leave these holy and historical places. They have no honor, no respect either for themselves or for our history. See what secularism has done to the Jewish soul."

The sociologist of religion Peter Berger has referred to contemporary religious communities who affirm literal biblical truths and a particular sacred history as "cognitive minorities."[2] The settlers are such a group, and as Berger explained, to be in a cognitive minority is psychologically unpleasant and problematic. People outside the group do not take you seriously. Seeing things so differently from most others and inhabiting a world where the past and present merge, as do the settlers, is not easy. Outsiders often take what you view as valuable and truthful to be entirely senseless fantasy. For many elite secular Israelis, the settlers are religious fanatics whose politics and activity have no rational justification and actually are the cause of continued conflict with the Palestinians. The Yesha explanations and justifications based upon history, cultural memory, faith, ongoing terrorism against Jewish targets, and the refusal of the Palestinian leaders to recognize Israel as a Jewish state are not taken seriously in important sectors of the Israeli academic and artistic elite. The settlers are seen by these elites as a danger to a modern democratic state. I was amazed during my research visits at the anger and visceral fury a discussion of the settlements elicited among opponents and otherwise mild-mannered secular Jews. During the summer of 2012, I visited an artist colony in Klil, situated in the hills of the Galilee in northern Israel. The residents were sophisticated and well-traveled people who had exhibited their work in the United States and Europe. They were friendly, open, warm, and hospitable. When my artist friend told them about my research with settlers, they became agitated and all protested that the settlers were the scourge of the country, ruining the economy and prolonging military service, and were immoral religious fanatics who wanted to turn the country into a theocracy where people like them had no place. One sculptor said, "I have nothing in common with those people, and if they get their way, I'm leaving the country." I tried to point out that while settler ideology was religious and based on their belief in the divine right of Jews to the Land of Israel, there was a fair argument to be made that no realistic peace with the Palestinians was currently possible given their militant Islamic stance and refusal to recognize the Jewishness of the state of Israel, something these Jewish artists greatly desired. I presented the Yesha view that unilaterally leaving territories occupied after the Six-Day War, as in the Gaza evacuation, actually invited greater militancy and increased attacks on Israel. There was no discussion. The consensus was that the settlers were cultists—"medievalists," one artist said—and these were people with whom one could not have a dialogue.

This attitude toward the settlers was not unusual. In the middle-class and politically moderate Samarian settlement of Kedumim, which is home to many educated professionals who commute to Tel Aviv and whose children seek university degrees, I met Alon Avineri, a young resident who was doing a PhD research project at the Hebrew University in Jerusalem under the direction of a renowned Israeli chemist. This chemist would argue with Alon about his living in an "illegal" settlement and indicated to him that his future academic appointments could be jeopardized by his residence in the occupied West Bank. Alon was quite an apolitical person and, though born and raised in Kedumim and committed to Jewish settlement, was not involved in political issues. Rather than jeopardize his future career, he decided to use a maternal aunt's Tel Aviv address while completing his doctorate. I, too, as a foreign academic, was viewed with suspicion because I was visiting settlements and was seen as somehow giving legitimacy to the settlement enterprise. This discomfort with the settlers extends even to their secular national supporters, who fervently back the settlement communities, not for theological reasons, but because they see them as legitimately Israeli territory necessary for national defense. Arieh Stav, who is head of the rightist think tank Ariel Center for Policy Research and the editor of the nationalist journal *Nativ*, is known as one of the most influential secular supporters of the settlements; nonetheless, knowing of my research, he asked me, "What's with their religion, singing and praying all the time. They live in another world, and they invite me to speak but I never feel quite comfortable with them."[3]

THE YESHA ENCLAVE CULTURE

As Berger has shown, to maintain their sense of identity and cohesion, "cognitive minorities" like the Yesha community must separate themselves from others and construct a society and culture where their alternative view of reality reigns supreme. This means establishing a separate network of social relations where the alternate view is taken for granted and members avoid interacting with outsiders. Living in an alternative reality has necessitated that the Yesha community construct special enclaves, physically, psychologically, and sociologically, to separate themselves from those hostile to their worldview and to associate chiefly with those who share their emotional and religious connection to the Land of Israel. Most Yesha communities—there are exceptions— are composed of residents who are strictly Orthodox and Sabbath observing. The Jewish Sabbath, a day of leisure for secular Israeli families, spent traveling, going to the beach, and visiting relatives, is in Yesha settlements a day of synagogue attendance and no work or travel and is a day spent having family meals, praying, and studying sacred texts. From Friday evening—the beginning of the Jewish Sabbath—to sundown Saturday, no automobiles enter or leave the settlements and no electronic devices are activated. It is a day of rest in accordance with strict Orthodox Halacha. Gender roles and family norms also follow strict Orthodox practice, and these rules strongly differentiate Yesha life from the lives of non-Orthodox Israelis. There are widely accepted religious norms regarding *tzniut*, modesty, in dress and gender interaction. Women wear special head coverings and loose-fitting dresses. Men have more leeway in dress—most dress in long trousers and dress shirts—but all wear the knitted kipah head covering that is a sign of settler loyalty. Unlike their Haredi sisters, Yesha women dress with color and even with an acceptable restrained flamboyance. Social dancing between men and women is not permitted, and men and women do not have physical contact unless they are married. Gender separation is the norm in the synagogue and in most social occasions. There is little interaction with secular Israelis outside of work contacts, and any type of interaction is problematic due to the gender rules and kosher laws prohibiting Orthodox setters from dining in a nonobservant home or restaurant.

Education from early childhood through high school is religious and community based and always under the aegis of Yesha rabbis and segregated by gender. The curriculum is based on religious Zionist teachings, which are presented as the Jewish norm. Both boys and girls study biblical and religious texts in depth, but only the boys study Talmudic literature, seen as the core of Jewish scholarship, in depth. Unlike their Haredi counterparts, both boys and girls receive secular instruction in English, advanced mathematics, and a range of humanistic studies. Many Yesha young people go on to university after they complete their army service. Prior to army service, Yesha young men (who usually serve in specially segregated units while attending an advanced yeshiva) attend a *mechina*, or preparatory academy, which readies them for the physical rigors of army service as well as interaction with nonsettler Israelis who might challenge their religiosity or messianic Zionism.[4] Some settler young women go into regular army units, but most serve in special national service units that limit their interaction with regular army recruits. It is, therefore, possible that a young person growing up in Hebron, Ofra, Kedumim, or another settlement will not have had any serious interaction with someone of their own age outside of the Yesha world. Entering the army or subsequently the workplace is challenging, as it is one of the few times that residents must face a disbelieving and sometimes hostile world. For the Yesha faithful, interacting with people outside the group is often unpleasant, difficult, and sometimes threatening or dangerous. Secular Israelis see them as religious fanatics, "fundamentalists" who stand in the way of a two-state solution that in their view would bring an end to the ongoing conflict and terror between Palestinians and Israelis. Their Orthodox beliefs and lifestyle are derided as primitive and out of touch with the modern world. One Hebrew University professor, Moshe Zimmerman, went so far as to compare militant young settlers to the Nazi Hitler youth movement.[5] Some secular leftist communities in Israel follow the European boycott of products produced in the settlements in Judea and Samaria and will not purchase or sell products knowingly produced in the West Bank by Jewish-owned companies.[6]

Living in an enclave community certainly protects the faithful, but as Berger pointed out, the cognitive minority must also develop theories, rationales, explanations, and justifications to legitimate their worldview and negate the value of those who challenge their reality. Put differently, it is not enough for a beleaguered minority to argue that their position is correct, but they must demonstrate the error of those who challenge and demean them. Here the Yesha community and its rabbinical and intellectual leadership have successfully confronted their adversaries on the basis of practical politics and military defense.

The Yesha community has argued that opposition to the settlements is irrational and self-defeating.[7] Rather than standing in the way of peace, the settlements are the first line of defense for Israeli cities and towns in the 1948 armistice line. Given continued Arab militancy, the attacks now taking place in the West Bank areas would simply occur in Israel proper. Moreover, the return of some of the West Bank territory has not resulted in peace between the parties but has actually renewed violence and increased conflict. For the settlers, the Gaza evacuations and the Oslo Peace Accords have been public relations events without any gain in security or reduction in violence. The settlers have a ready explanation for the secular hostility to their settlement ideology. Secular Israelis are embarrassed about living in and having a Jewish state; they feel like impostors and colonialists. As religious Zionists put it, the only authentic right Jews have to the Land of Israel is religious and theological. God bequeathed the land in eternity to the Jewish people. Once this truth is not accepted, once divine promises are seen as mere myth, the Jewish right to the Land of Israel is lost. In the settler view, Jews who do not acknowledge the divine rights are ambivalent, confused, and defeatist. They are merely secular nationalists warring with another nationalist entity over ordinary land and territory. Their unease is not only with Judea and Samaria but with the whole Zionist enterprise. Yesha ideologists say their secular adversaries are guilt ridden; they lack confidence in the Jewish future and want to deny their Jewish identity and destiny. The truth, say many settlers, is that secular Israelis secretly believe the Palestinians are right and they, the Jews, are the usurpers of the land. Yesha communities contrast this confusion with their own certainty and faith. Settlers and religious Zionists are confident; they know God's plan, and if they remain strong in their belief and in their settlement activities, full Jewish sovereignty and redemption will take place. The settlers contrast their own confidence and willingness to sacrifice with what they see as the vacuity and confusion of secular Israel. "I am sad for them," said one young Hebron militant speaking of secular Israeli young people; "all they want is *chaim tovim*, a good time, discos and parties with their *hevra*, their buddies. Our goal is not to have a good time but to carry out God's plan."

RELIGIOUS NATIONALISM: AN AMBIVALENT LOYALTY

The Yesha settlers are fervent Israeli nationalists and deeply patriotic, but their loyalty to the state, so anchored in religious faith, sets them apart from the bulk of Israeli society. The state of Israel for them is not a secular entity but an emanation of divine providence, and religious Zionist settlers celebrate the state's day of independence, *Yom Ha'atzmaut*, as a religious holiday with special prayers and synagogue services. The state of Israel, however, is to be valued only insofar as it fulfills its purpose as a vessel for attaining Jewish sovereignty and encouraging the messianic process. The settler position, sometimes articulated but often an insider view, is that the state can depend on them to sacrifice for the defense of the country, to encourage their youth to volunteer for dangerous missions, and to be a bridge to the Christian Zionist lobby in the United States, but all this is contingent on cooperation with the agenda of religious Zionism. When on September 13, 1993, in front of the White House in Washington, DC, and with much fanfare, the Israeli government and the Palestinian Authority signed the Oslo Accords, which were to be the basis for a peace agreement that returned areas in Judea and Samaria to the Palestinian Authority, Rabbi Zalman Melamed and scores of settler leaders declared the agreement null and void. Giving up the ancestral lands in part of biblical Eretz Yisrael for any reason, including for peace, goes against the Torah. Melamed, one of the most outspoken Yesha rabbis, said plainly, "Anything that goes against the Torah is invalid." Melamed's position was and still is that in this time of a reborn Israel living in messianic times, there can be no secular politics; all state matters need rabbinical guidance and direction.[8] Politics and security are central to rabbinical leadership and are not to be left to secular state authorities alone. Rabbi Shlomo Aviner, in an essay condemning the Oslo Accords, saw the state's obsessive concern with seeking a peace agreement as short-sighted and self-defeating. The cessation of conflict is a laudable goal, he explained, but an authentic and theologically valid Jewish peace must further God's plans for Jewish sovereignty over the whole of the Land of Israel.[9] I heard over and over in my interviews the anger and frustration so many religious Zionists had for the secular government opposed to the settlements. "They are hardly Jews; they want a European state and not Jewish state," said some, or others, more understanding, would say, "We cannot condemn them; the Israeli educational system failed them, did not give them any Jewish content. They speak Hebrew but think like *Goyim*, Gentiles." Despite these sentiments, the settlers are enormously proud of Israeli high-tech accomplishments and their country's standing in the global economy; they talk about Israeli breakthroughs in medicine and science with great pride, and they are proud of their universities and even talk about Israeli artistic advances. And there are not a few settlers involved in these national accomplishments.

The Yesha ambivalence to the secular Zionist state and society has its basis in their version of religious Zionism. In this view, conceived and developed by Rabbi Avraham Yitzchak Kook (1886–1935), a celebrated Talmudist and cabalist who was influenced by the Hegelian view of history, it was secular and even rabidly antireligious Jews who through their secular Zionist activities were the unconscious and unwitting builders of the materialist foundations of the Jewish state to usher in the messianic age.[10] Once the secular, irreligious Jews prepared the physical conditions for the Jewish renaissance in the Holy Land, Kook believed the religious Orthodox Jews would continue building the state and see the messianic process to fruition. The secular Zionist unbelievers were critical to the historical messianic process and were unknowing allies in the religious quest for messianic redemption. Kook, who was fervently Orthodox, dressed in traditional eastern European garb, opposed modern culture, and was a supporter of a theocratic Jewish state, was nonetheless a supporter of secular Zionism, once proclaiming Theodor Herzl a proto-messianic figure. Secular political Zionism, however, was to be a transitory phase to be superseded by religious Zionism, which would lead to the historical endpoint of a theocratic state

worthy of messianic redemption. Kook the elder and later his son, Rabbi Tzvi Yehuda Kook, who elaborated his father's philosophy, bequeathed this Hegelian outlook to the settler movement. The secular
Zionist government of the state of Israel is important and of great value,
but religious Zionist loyalty is contingent upon their historical duty in
laying the groundwork for a religious commonwealth. The settlers, following Tzvi Yehuda Kook, see deep and enduring value in the secular
state, but their support is compromised when the government refuses
to support religious Zionist goals and impedes the fulfillment of Jewish
historical destiny. Some elements in the religious Zionist camp associated with the more mystical outlook of Rabbi Tzvi Tau of the Har Hamor
Yeshiva community go further in their commitment to the state of Israel as a vehicle of messianic redemption. In Tau's view, the state,
despite all its imperfections and corruption, represents the soul of the
Jewish nation and is essential to the ultimate redemption. Tau and his
followers are staunchly nationalistic and reject Western culture and
modern secularism, but oppose the aggressive politics and civil disobedience associated with parts of the Yesha movement. [11]

This is an ongoing dilemma in the religious Zionist Yesha community. What is the religiously appropriate response to the state? Is the
state, with all its flaws, its refusal to adopt Halacha as the sole law of the
land, its opposition to the Yesha settlement agenda, and its willingness
to evacuate and even destroy existing settlements, to be held up as the
carrier of messianic promise? The bulk of settlers are committed to the
state and to the political process, seeing the current situation as leading
to an eventual historical synthesis as outlined in Kookian philosophy.
For these activists, aggressive Yesha politics and tactics and settlement
expansion keep the state on the right track to messianic redemption.
When I challenged the rabbi of a settlement in the Samarian region
about the lack of popular or government support and questioned
whether the state is indeed furthering the Yesha agenda—the Israeli
government had recently sent in the military to destroy the few make-
shift buildings for a new illegal outpost that would have expanded his
settlement—he quickly responded, "Things come slowly, people are
becoming more religious, and it's just a matter of time when things will
occur as expected, but we must persevere and always have *bitachon*,
faith in our goals."

Some settler groups have retreated from their strong identification with the state of Israel and have adopted a more Haredi pacifist outlook, refusing to enlist in the Israeli army and not observing Zionist state holidays, no longer seeing the current state as an authentic harbinger of messianic transformation. Still others, such as Rabbis Aron Lichtenstein and Yehudah Amital of the Har Etzion Yesha, located in the occupied West Bank, represent the moderate wing of the movement and remain committed to the religious Zionist agenda while opposing the mainline Yesha politics of civil disobedience and opposition to the government. This group believes in gradualism, compromise, and always respecting governmental authority. Lichtenstein, a famed American Talmudic scholar with a PhD in literature from Harvard University, and Amital, who came to Israel after experiencing the Holocaust in Europe, are both strong Zionists, but their positions on messianic gradualism and political compromise—they supported territorial exchange—put them at odds with much of the Yesha rank and file. Lichtenstein, though very much a faithful Zionist, has argued that Yesha settlement politics and tactics must be accepted by the bulk of Israeli society, and as this is not the case currently, moderation and limitation on settlement agitation is necessary in order to maintain social and political order and civility.[12] The religious Zionism of Amital and Lichtenstein and their followers supports the settler movement and acknowledges the messianic potentiality of the state of Israel, but their messianism is muted, patient, and they are willing to defer to the public will and to governmental policy.

DIASPORA JEWS AND SETTLER JEWS

The settlers see themselves as the "new" Jews, proud, unafraid, courageous, and reborn in the sanctity of the Holy Land, residing in the sacred precincts of Judea and Samaria, in the very dwelling places of the ancient patriarchs and prophets. They are the contemporary *chalutzim*, pioneers, the guardians of the Holy Land, God's infantry who are fighting for the realization of Jewish sovereignty in the Land of Israel as foretold in sacred scripture. The settlers see themselves as righting historical wrongs, making history, and asserting Jewish honor and power. They are, in their own view, undoing the psychic and relig-

ious damage done to Jews and Judaism in the course of the long diaspora experience as a demeaned, powerless, and stateless people. This
takes guts, a willingness to suffer the rejection of the international community and even their own brethren, who through timidity and fear
accept outsider status and inferiority and see the settlers as troublemak-
ers who elicit hostility and violence against Jews all over the world.[13]
Jews who reject Yesha Zionism and settlement activity are rejecting
Jewish destiny and chosenness and identifying with their oppressors.

In the Yesha view, *Galut* Jews, those living outside of Israel, are
afraid of living in a free and independent Jewish nation, preferring
homelessness to taking responsibility and asserting their Jewish identity
and destiny. Diaspora Jews live in perpetual fear as outsiders in foreign
lands, seeking to curry favor with government officials, always kowtow-
ing and living with little self-respect. No matter how long these Jews
have resided outside the Land of Israel, whether in Europe, the Middle
East, or even the United States, they are always seen as alien and never
as truly native to their diaspora homes. Diaspora Jews have become
wealthy and educated, even rising to elite positions in their host countries, but always at the cost of losing their Jewish identity and ultimately
assimilating to their host environments. In the final settler analysis,
most diaspora Jews will be lost to the Jewish community. High rates of
intermarriage—in some diaspora communities, three-quarters of Jews
marry people of another faith, and the vast majority of their offspring do
not identify with the Jewish people—and growing secularization have
resulted in a severely diminished Jewish population outside of Israel.
For settlers, there is no Jewish future outside the state of Israel.[14]

Traditionally, Orthodox Jews in insular diaspora communities do not
intermarry and remain attached to Jewish tradition and faith. Still, religious Zionist settlers see these Jews as disloyal to the call to settlement
and residence in the Land of Israel. The error of these deeply pious
Jews is their refusal to recognize that the divine call to the Jewish
people was not individual observance or even a pariah communal existence in alien lands but the establishment of a national community and
sacred nation living in the precincts of Eretz Yisrael. Jewish law is clear,
writes Rabbi Shlomo Aviner, following the classical rabbinical view:
living in Israel is obligatory for every Jew, and residence in the Land of
Israel is the same as if all of God's commandments were followed.
Living in Israel is a religious obligation of the highest sort, and Jews

who remain apart are violating a central Jewish commandment. The determination among some Haredi Jews to remain ensconced in the diaspora is not only a violation of religious law but a fatal flaw in their theological outlook. Judaism is not just a religious community with beliefs, rituals, and ceremonies but a nation commanded to live in a specific land with a distinct culture and lifestyle, an army and an economy, that will be a beacon of hope and light to all humankind. The divine Jewish mission can only be fulfilled in the Land of Israel, the specific and unique place that God has given in perpetuity to the Jewish people. Jews who refuse to come home, to be part of the national renaissance, have domesticated and reduced the universalist mission of the Jewish nation. Such Jews are living a flawed existence as a homeless and unwanted people and, even more significantly, have been disobedient to God's call to return to Zion.[15]

The term *Galuti*, a person of the diaspora, is used in settler jargon not only for Jews living abroad but derisively for Israelis, whether religious or secular, who do not acknowledge the new reality of the state of Israel, Jewish military and political power, and the new psychology of autonomy and potency that was lost in the long sojourn of the diaspora. To the Zionist settlers, the Israeli secular left, particularly those adamantly opposed to the settlements in Judea and Samaria, are still beset by an unwarranted diaspora mentality of fear and anxiety of the international community. They still think of Jews as a weak people, are deeply conflicted about the Zionist enterprise of independence and military might, and express shame and guilt over Jewish victory and territorial expansion. For the settlers, the Israeli left are Jews living in the Land of Israel but psychologically still in the diaspora, afraid of Gentile disapproval, which leads them to a naïve belief in compromise and territorial surrender.

An essential element of settler culture and psychology is the rejection of the Galut mentality of compromise and avoidance of confrontation and violence. In contrast, the settlers urge confronting danger and attacks from enemies. "We are not in a European country here," one young Jewish militant told me when I asked about several incidents of rocks thrown at settler cars near the Yitzhar settlement. "We know how to take care of ourselves," he said somewhat cryptically, and I knew this meant going into adjacent Palestinian villages and uprooting olive groves. All of the settlements have their own defense groups, and there

is a culture of toughness and physical confrontation between the settlers and the local Palestinians so unlike the traditional Jewish culture of
passivity, surrender, and escape. Young settlers with no experience or
little memory of the Jewish Galut experience are particularly adamant
that the settlements are Jewish land and that military might and violent
confrontation are to be used to protect Jews in the whole of the Land of
Israel. In this sense, the Yesha movement is as much about religious
faith as it is about Jewish psychological transformation.

"A DANGEROUS NEIGHBORHOOD": PALESTINIANS AND JEWISH SETTLERS

Daily life for Jews in Judea and Samaria is dangerous. Palestinian militants engage in rock throwing at moving vehicles, stabbings, murders,
and suicide bombings. Every settlement I visited had a story to tell
about an attack on the road or the murder of a settlement family.
Settlers feel deeply misunderstood by the Israeli left, by the bulk of
American Jews, and by the international community, who refuse to
recognize the everyday danger and hostility faced by the settlers. "Let's
face it," one American-born settler in the village of Ofra told me after a
series of attacks on a family where the father and one brother were
killed, "we are not living in Iowa or Connecticut; this is the Middle
East, where you fight back or are killed." Era Rapaport, an American-
born and -trained social worker who immigrated to Israel and became
the mayor of the Shiloh settlement, tells how in his first years of residence he believed that negotiation with the local Palestinian population
would stop attacks on the settlement water supply and phone lines. But
despite repeated attempts and good interaction with the local *mukhtar*,
the Palestinian village head, the attacks and raids continued. His colleagues, knowing his American origins, demanded that he stop negotiations and conduct retaliatory raids. They explained, "You are trying to
introduce Western values into an Oriental/Middle Eastern society. It
won't work." Rapaport, seeing the failure of negotiation, came to see
violent retaliation as necessary in the context of conflict between settlers and Palestinian militants and was eventually jailed for attacks on
Palestinians.[16]

The settler view of Arabs is deeply complex and varied. The settlers are apprehensive about the Arab population—about 20 percent of the population within the pre-1967 armistice lines are Arab, and Arabs account for about one million of the residents of the West Bank—but their concerns and attitudes are nationalistic and not racist. The settlers as a group are respectful of Islam as an authentic monotheistic religion and the one most closely akin to Judaism, distinguishing it from Christianity, which some rabbinical commentators view as compromising strict monotheism. There are also considerable cultural commonalities between Islam and Orthodox Judaism in modesty regulations, family life, prayer schedules, theological reflections, and even elements of food preparation and diet. Settlers always insist that they are culturally and religiously closer to the Islamic community than the secular Israeli groups, who see the settlers as racists. And some settlement leaders, rabbis, and communities have established cooperative relations with local Palestinians.[17]

Still, religion, sovereignty, and territory are at the heart of the continuing conflict. Religious Zionist settlers insist on their central theological view that the whole biblical Land of Israel was a divine bequest to the Jewish people alone and not to be shared with any other people or nation. This is not negotiable. Moreover, they say, there never was a Palestinian nation anywhere in the territory of the Holy Land. For hundreds of years prior to 1948, Arabs and others living in what was then referred to as Palestine were part of the Turkish Ottoman Empire and had no standing as a distinct sovereign entity. Palestine was part of an Ottoman district known as Greater Syria. When the British mandate began in Palestine, there was no Palestinian entity, and even after 1948, when the British left and a territory was carved out to be a Palestinian state, the Arabs living in the West Bank did not form a separate national entity but became citizens of the Hashemite Kingdom of Jordan. Much of the West Bank is still unpopulated, and there is ample room for all groups to live there. In the Yesha view, there never was a distinct Palestinian entity, demands for a Palestinian state have no historical or legal legitimacy, and agitation for Palestinian statehood is just camouflage for the real goal of eliminating the state of Israel. The Yesha position was stated clearly by the movement's charismatic founder, Tzvi Yehuda Kook, and despite emendations and reinterpretation, it remains the dominant Yesha worldview:

It is imperative to know that we are not obligated to give the Arabs any sovereignty over this land. As individuals, they can remain here as a minority. If they do not cause us any trouble, and do not rebel against our rule, but accept our sovereignty over this Land, then we won't trouble them. It is important to speak with them, to explain, to convince, and to endeavor to lessen the animosity between Arabs and Jews; to increase friendly and closer relations; and to eliminate all discrimination—but first, it must be clear that this is our land, from the beginning of time to the end! *On this point, there is nothing to discuss.* [18]

Kook's position is based on the biblical accounts of Holy War undertaken by the ancient Israelites as they entered the Promised Land and battled the Canaanites. These wars and killings recounted in the Hebrew Bible were necessary, according to rabbinical and Talmudic judgment, because they purged the Holy Land of idol worshippers and pagans. However, those Canaanites who renounced paganism and followed what the Talmudic rabbis considered to be the basic human morality of the monotheistic Noahide codes, were allowed to remain. [19] The Palestinians are viewed from this theological prism. So long as Jewish sovereignty is accepted and there is allegiance to the Jewish state of Israel, Palestinians have a place. In the settler view, Palestinian Arabs have rights as citizens, but allegiance and acceptance of the inherent Jewishness of the state and the legitimacy of sole Jewish sovereignty over the entire Land of Israel is a necessary condition for residence and civil rights.

This is the public theological view, and it is not a novel Yesha position but a classical Jewish one codified in Halachic literature. The reality of everyday life and politics, however, is one of enmity, conflict, violent confrontation, bombings, suicide attacks, and land disputes. The Palestinians understandably see the settlers as conquerors, interlopers who have taken their land and deprived them of their national destiny, and have no desire to live as "guests" in what they consider their native land. Palestinians engaging in violence and terror are not immoral criminals but are acting morally and religiously in resistance to an alien conqueror. Rock throwing, bombing, and civilian attacks are legitimate activities taken against a well-armed alien state enemy. To the Muslim faithful, particularly in the traditional areas of the West Bank such as Hebron and Nablus, the Jewish settlers are an assault on Dar al-Islam, the territory of Islam, conquered and settled by Muslim faithful, and this Muslim land is never to be under the domination of non-Muslim authority. The view of traditional orthodox Islam is clear: Palestine is a valid Islamic territory that is not to be ceded to a foreign nation or religion. The Yesha view is that the Palestinians cannot and will not, given their religious faith, accept a sovereign Jewish state in Palestine. Consequently, any attempt to end the conflict at this time is a Western illusion based on ignorance of Islamic texts and religious culture. As one Yesha leader explained, peaceful relations with the Arab community are not possible because "peace with non-Muslims contradicts their beliefs." For the settlers, the Arabs remain the enemy, and conflict and confrontation are the reality. Both sides, it appears, can justify their claims in stark theological terms, and these religious motivations continue to foster enmity and violence.[20]

RELIGION, VIOLENCE, AND MARTYRDOM

Given the furious disagreement over sacred territory between Israelis and Palestinians, violence is almost a daily and unsurprising occurrence. Living and traveling in the West Bank is dangerous, and all Jewish residents are open to bomb attacks, suicide bombers, sniper fire, and rock throwing. Jewish residents carry firearms and live with the understanding that the area is contested and that a de facto state of war exists between Arabs and Jews. To the Yesha Zionist settlers, the area is the biblical Judea and Samaria promised to the Jewish people for eternity, the place where their biblical forefathers lived and the sacred events of Jewish history took place. For these faithful Jewish believers, the hills are saturated with Jewish history and are the sites of divine revelations and holy war, and remain a sacred and cherished inheritance never to be forsaken. In the settler view, there is no occupation but a homecoming.

For Islam as well, these areas are sacred and an essential part of the *Ummah*, the Muslim world community faithful to the *sharia*, the Muslim religious canon, and governed by the wisdom and learning of established religious authorities. In Islamic religious understanding, once an area has become part of the Islamic world, it is considered Muslim and should rightfully remain an integral part of the Ummah. The Palestinian

Holy Land with its sacred Muslim sites, including the Ibrahimi mosque in Hebron and the Haram el-Sharif in East Jerusalem, where the Prophet Mohammed is believed to have ascended to heaven, are now under alien Israeli control. These lands and territories in orthodox Muslim teaching may never be ceded to non-Muslim authority, and a sacred war may be declared to oust those occupying Muslim land and regain sovereignty. In the words of a Muslim scholar and professor of Islamic studies, the Jewish state must be "dismantled" and a war fought against "the Zionist army, state and its public institutions" until Islamic control is established over the whole of the Holy Land.[21] Some Muslim authorities might disagree with an imminent Holy War, but significant elements and respectable Muslim authorities condone religious violence against Israeli control of the West Bank. Both sides can and do quote their sacred scriptures, either Torah or Quran, to justify their claims and in seeing the ensuing hostility as decreed by religious faith and doctrine.[22]

There have been hundreds of attacks on Israeli settlers and travelers in the West Bank territories, either on the roadways or directly on settlement families in their own homes. One of these home attacks that attracted international attention was the killing of Udi and Ruth Fogel and their three children as they slept in their home in the settlement of Itamar on the Sabbath eve.[23] There are confrontations, rock throwing, and gun battles every day in the West Bank—many of them unreported—between local Palestinians and settlers, and scores of people, including children, have been killed on both sides.[24] The danger to life is certainly frightening, but the ongoing conflict and the lack of personal security must also raise critical questions about the nature of the settlement enterprise and by extension the success and even validity of Zionism and the Jewish return to their Holy Land. The goal of Zionism was for a Jewish homeland where the Jews would be a normal people, a normal nation, free of persecution and safe from violence. This clearly has not occurred.

There have been attacks on Israeli civilians—and these continue—within the 1948 border lines, but the bulk of attacks and terror now take place in the contested West Bank, and all acknowledge that there is serious danger in these contested areas. The emphasis on preserving human life is paramount in Jewish law and theology with few exceptions; all religious strictures, rituals, and Halachic rules can be violated to preserve human life. A Jew, even among the most ultra-Orthodox, may, for example, violate the Sabbath or eat nonkosher food if life is in danger. Life triumphs religious law except in cases of forced conversion to idolatry or an order to commit murder or engage in sexually deviant acts. Knowing the value and standing of life in Jewish culture, I was intrigued by the ready acceptance of danger in the settlements. In one of my visits to an outpost—actually one large house surrounded by Israeli armored vehicles near the main settlement in Hebron—that was the site of daily attacks by local militants, I asked one of the residents, a mother of ten children, the youngest an infant girl, "Why put your kids in such danger; you are being shot at and cannot leave without an armed guard?" The young mother, a daughter-in-law of Rabbi Moshe Levinger, one of the founders of Hebron, casually explained, "This is our land; we have to take control, and this is our duty and fate. This is what God wants of us."

I heard similar responses in other settlements where tragedy had occurred. In Ofra, near Jerusalem, a father and son were killed in terrorist attacks within weeks of each other, and during a memorial service I attended, the surviving nine-year-old son and brother said the Kaddish memorial prayers. People were deeply moved and many were in tears, but when the ceremony was concluded, the settlement leaders announced that killings would only spur them on to build more houses and apartments in honor of those they called the *Kedoshim*, religious martyrs.[25] Geula Cohen, a famed member of the radical militant Stern Group, which carried out guerrilla attacks on British soldiers in Mandate Palestine and who moved in old age to live in Hebron, explained to an interviewer that compromise and peace settlements are not Zionist goals. "Our goal was to settle the Land of Israel. Of course no one wants his children to go to war and risk their lives but unfortunately we are living in a time of war that requires sacrifice. It has been our destiny since our forefather Jacob fought with the angel during which his hip got injured and thereafter walked with a limp. That's how it is. There can be no tomorrow if we do not pay a price for it."[26]

Martyrdom and the willingness to offer one's life for God and for Jewish destiny and honor has deep biblical roots in Judaism. The Hebrew Bible records the story of the patriarch Abraham, who is commanded, as a show of faith, to offer his much-beloved son Isaac as a sacrifice. Both father and son go along with God's directives and are ready to complete the sacrificial offering when at the last moment a heavenly voice instructs them to substitute an animal sacrifice. This narrative, referred to in Jewish theology as *Akedath Yitzchak*, the binding of Isaac, serves as the quintessential example of pure faith and has become the model of Jewish martyrdom through the ages. The binding of Isaac has come to mean that God, in his mystery and grandeur, will at times desire that the faithful sacrifice their lives in his honor and can demand the death of the innocent. The lesson learned from Abraham's willingness to sacrifice his beloved son is that life is not the ultimate value; rather, obedience and unquestioning faith in divine providence are demanded of the faithful Jew.

Perhaps the most prominent example of Jewish martyrdom is the story of the mass suicides in 70 CE at Masada, a mountain fortification in the Judean desert. There, for three years, 960 Jews were surrounded by Roman soldiers during the Judean revolt against the Romans, who controlled Judea. As the Romans finally breached the walls of the Masada encampment, the inhabitants committed suicide rather than be taken prisoner by their Roman enemies.[27] The Masada story continues to animate Jewish martyrdom, self-sacrifice, and religious nationalism. Elite units of the Israeli Defense Forces are inducted during candle-lighting ceremonies at Masada, where they take vows of office at the sacred site. Yesha has continued this tradition, which gives sacred meaning to the attacks and deaths experienced in terrorist incidents. The theme of suffering and martyrdom is an essential part of Yesha culture and theology. In this view, settling the Land of Israel, residing in the contested and dangerous areas of biblical Judea and Samaria, never ceding any part of biblical Israel, never permitting non-Jews to have sovereignty in any part of Eretz Yisrael, are religious obligations that transcend human life. Those who are killed are Kedoshim, sacred martyrs who gave their lives to secure Jewish sovereignty in the Land of Israel.

RELIGION AND HOLY WAR

The settler movement and its rabbinical leadership see war, violence, and martyrdom as necessary and religious components of Jewish sovereignty and the unfolding of the messianic process. Yesha theology claims that current conditions mandate a *Milchemet Mitzvah*, an obligatory holy war against Israel's enemies, with all its attendant violence and loss of life, to secure Jewish sovereignty and expand Jewish settlement in the whole of the Land of Israel.[28] In the Yesha view, this is not a theological innovation or a departure from traditional Rabbinical Judaism but an essential expectation elaborated in biblical, Talmudic, and rabbinical literature. The fact that Jews historically have not engaged in war and violent confrontation was a result of fear, homelessness, and statelessness. They were weak, a pariah people, passive and timid, without the necessary military power to wage war. This was the past. The new reality of the Jewish state has now allowed Jews and Judaism to fulfill their mission to reclaim their full homeland with the weapons of war. In this view, Jewish holy war is a divine decree and a moral imperative because Jewish settlement and sovereignty partakes of a higher moral calculus, one anchored in divine truth.[29] Yesha theology argues that the return of Jewish people to the Holy Land, though involving war, violence, and dislocation, will come to be seen as a wondrous event for all humankind, as these events will result in messianic transformation.

The clearest statement of this view was made by the charismatic Tzvi Yehuda Kook and later elaborated by his many students. Kook explained that a war for Eretz Yisrael was a mitzvah like any other mitzvah, and Jews had to come to terms with Jewish power, war, and violence as religious obligations.

> The Ramban clearly determines that conquering the Land of Israel to ensure Jewish sovereignty is the *Milchemet Mitzvah*, holy war, of the Torah. This is a precept of the Torah and there is no getting around it. There is no nation without a land, and the concrete, living, here and now Israel is compelled to hold on to its land. This precept continues in each generation and the Ramban emphasizes three times. In previous generations, including generations of Tzaddikim, we did not fulfill this mitzvah. Why? Because we were in a situation where, against our will, we could not. . . . Today we have the weapons of war and this precept has returned to our hands. Torah, war and settlement are three sides of a triangle. And how incredibly privileged we are to be assertive in all.[30]

Kook's words on the religious nature of holy war to secure Jewish settlement were written over forty years ago and have undergone re-interpretation and refinement but still remain at the center of Yesha ideology. The "liberal" settler establishment, usually living in large city-like blocs like Efrat in Gush Etzion or Kedumim in the Shomron, see war and violent reprisal for Arab terror and attacks as necessary but think the state is the sole legitimate entity to carry these out. They see vigilante reprisal as dangerous and disruptive to maintaining an orderly and moral society. One young settler, a lawyer who commuted to work in Jerusalem, living in a small settlement in the Shomron where homes were periodically set on fire by Arab militants, agreed with this position and told me, "We suffer greatly from arson attacks from the local Arab villagers but we decided not to take action in our own hands. We have an army and a strong police; let them do their job. Friends from other settlements see us as weak and just leaving ourselves open to further attacks, but we think this is the moral and religious way to go." Other settlers, in areas where there is more militancy, often see the government response as weak and halfhearted. These settlers believe the Is-raeli government, under pressure from opponents of the settlement enterprise and from the international community, has not sufficiently defended the settlements and tolerates Palestinian violence without re-sponding with military or police action. In some of these communities, new self-defense groups have been formed, and these groups, without governmental sanction, retaliate against Palestinians they know or sus-pect have carried out attacks. These groups engage in what has been termed "price tag" attacks, meaning the settlers extract a "price" in life or property for any attack on a Yesha settlement. Price tag violence is an ongoing phenomenon and has resulted in a spiraling of intergroup vio-lence as each group responds and mutual violence continues.[31]

It is important to recognize that the Yesha theology of Jewish power and confrontation, and the justification of violence and the value of religious martyrdom, are not innovations but are based on classical rab-binical texts, universally studied in yeshiva seminaries and accepted as an integral part of the Halachic canon. The sole Jewish right to the Land of Israel, the right and obligation of war and violence in pursuit of Jewish sovereignty, and laws of vengeance are all clearly articulated in rabbinical literature. What the Yesha movement has done is show that these sacred texts, once merely studied during the millennia the Jews were a homeless and powerless people, have now become the actual policy and program of religious Zionism. It is important for scholars and diplomats to recognize theology and cultural memory as forces in the Israeli–Palestinian conflict, because texts long thought irrelevant and ignored can be rediscovered and animate the religious faithful. In this regard, Yesha rabbis are not incorrect when they claim that they are fully faithful to the Torah and the rabbinical tradition in their pursuit of Jewish settlement and sovereignty in the Land of Israel.

War and Judaism have been seen by both by Jews and non-Jews alike as polar opposites. Messianic Zionism has resuscitated older holy war doctrines and has in this way transformed contemporary religious Zionism, maintaining that "war is also the beginning of redemption."[32] This theological position animates settler politics, religion, and culture. Again it is Rabbi Kook who first articulated this holy war doctrine:

> If it were possible to conquer the land without spilling blood, certainly this would be better. This is obvious. However, until the "end of days" when *nation shall not lift up sword against nation*, sometimes we have to act with our soldiers and army. We actualize the commandment, to hold the Land of Israel in our hands, and not leave it under the rule of any other nation through our military action, even in the light of the unpleasant consequences which war involves. . . . As explained by the Ramban this Land must be in our hands, under our sovereignty and government, and not under the rule of any other nation.[33]

The decorated paratrooper, ordained rabbi, and diligent Kook student Hanan Porat explained to settler opponents that ultimately there is no contradiction between warring to settle the land and peace: "The message of peace will only come from the Mountain of the House of God—from the rebuilt Temple." It is messianic world transformation that will defeat "the craving for power and pride" and will bring world peace and harmony.[34]

Considering these Talmudic and Halachic positions on Jewish sovereignty and the sacredness of war in pursuit of these goals, it is incorrect to claim that the Yesha movement does not have a firm basis in normative Jewish law and theology for their political and theological agenda. This does not mean that all Jewish theologians and communal leaders identify with Yesha goals and politics. Indeed, establishment rabbinical

and lay Jewish leaders in both Israel and the United States are opposed
to Yesha militancy. The Yesha movement is criticized and rejected for a
variety of reasons; some argue that their program of bellicose politics
leads to war, and some have opposed the movement on ethical grounds,
that it is immoral in denying Palestinian rights to a national homeland,
but one cannot legitimately make the claim that the Yesha movement
does not have a firm basis in Talmudic texts and in the normative Jewish
Halachic legal tradition. The absolute right of Jewish residence and
sovereignty in the Land of Israel is so deeply embedded in Jewish
history, religious culture, and theological formulation that despite the
radical nature of Yesha, it can legitimately claim religious authenticity
and fealty to Jewish history and self-understanding.

The theoretical Talmudic arguments for settlements and Jewish sovereignty I discovered in the settlement rabbinical literature impressed
me as authentic and true to the world of rabbinical and Halachic disputation, but how could this age-old view be reconciled with the political
realities of the contemporary world? What of the Palestinians living for
centuries in the lands claimed by the settlers? What of the more than
one million Palestinians who similarly claimed the West Bank lands as
their national home? Should a state of war and conflict continue indefi-
nitely in defense of an age-old biblical promise? I decided to put these
questions to political leaders, rabbis, and ordinary settlers, and I report
on these conversations in the next chapter.

4

INSIDE THE SETTLEMENTS: PORTRAITS, CONVERSATIONS, AND EXPERIENCES

A PARTICIPANT OBSERVER

Doing participant observation and reporting on life and faith in Yesha settlement communities is complex, problematic, and controversial. The most deeply committed settlers believed that, as an American academic, I was an outsider who could not appreciate nor fully understand their deep literal faith and their willingness for self-sacrifice. Sometimes called radicals or extremists, these settlers were generally cordial and surprisingly open about their beliefs regarding Jewish sovereignty. They openly acknowledged seeing themselves as a religious avant-garde whose efforts will restore a Jewish theocracy and lead to world messianic transformation. They were frank about their disenchantment with modernity—its emphasis on individualism, permissiveness, secularism, and sexual modernism and feminist ideology—which they thought destroyed religious faith and the traditional family. While these more ideologically committed settlers constantly and honestly invoked the Bible and rabbinical literature as justification for their settlement and opposition to the Israeli government, they felt I could never fully understand and identify with their life and culture.

Surprisingly, it was the more moderate, usually secularly educated, but also ideological settlers who were the most difficult to interview and the least forthcoming. Discussions of a coming theocracy and messianic transformation were met with silence or denial. I knew from their theo-

logical tracts that messianism and theocracy were at the center of the
Yesha worldview and that both Tzvi Yehuda Kook and his father Avraham Yitzhak Kook had placed these at the center of religious Zionism.
Nonetheless, in the educated middle-class settlements, the emphasis
was on the beauty of the land and its restoration as a Jewish commonwealth, and questions of messianism and violence were considered irrelevant. I had a good command of the rabbinical literature and at times
I would challenge people I met, giving counter-texts. On occasion, I
would get agreement about messianic aspirations, but more often on
politically sensitive topics I was told, "You are an American; you really
do not know the way things operate in Israel." When I insisted that
violence was increasing in some extremist settlements to the degree
that some young radicals were considering killing Israeli soldiers on
social media, I was told this was just talk or that the young people were
defending their homes and all this was taken out of context.[1]

The secular Israeli opposition to the settlement enterprise reacted to
me quite differently. Those deeply opposed to the settlement program
and to its faith-based politics thought I was taken in by the settlers and
that writing about them in what they saw as a nonjudgmental or sympathetic way would give the "crazies," as they were often called, credence
in the Western press and in academic circles. One former military intelligence officer said to me, "These people are ruining the country, and
you are giving them a platform to gain respectability. If you want to
write about them, read *The Settlers* by an Israeli journalist and follow
up on the danger they represent."[2] I was surprised at how few secular
Israelis had ever been to a West Bank settlement and how little they
knew about religious Zionist faith and culture.[3] Still, their curiosity was
great, and I was constantly asked to report on what I saw and experienced.

Within the Yesha movement, I found considerable diversity. There
were differences between moderates and radicals, between active messianists and gradualists, and between communities who support vigilante defense and those who look to state authority. However, the Yesha
movement as a whole does share a political and religious stance on a
Jewish state in the whole of the biblical Land of Israel. All involved in
the movement believe in Jewish rights to Judea and Samaria, but some
oppose any territorial compromise and engage in violent defense of
their settlements. Others disagree, believing that despite ideology and

faith some territorial exchanges, while painful, are legitimate in the short term in the pursuit of a peace agreement and the cessation of Palestinian attacks. Some settlers are fierce messianists wanting to usher in the messianic era immediately and to construct a new Temple along the lines of the ancient one destroyed almost two thousand years ago, complete with animal sacrifices. Others claim that the Messiah will come "little by little" and the times are just not ready for Temple construction.[4] Still others, fervent believers that the messianic process is occurring, want to mute their messianic goals so as not to antagonize secular Israelis and the international community. Some so-called settlements encircling Jerusalem have been incorporated into metropolitan Jerusalem and people living there do not necessarily see themselves as ideological settlers but want to live a comfortable suburban life in an attractive but relatively inexpensive area. In all settlement areas, whether in Judea, Samaria, or in the Jerusalem suburbs, Yesha has a strong following and residents identify with the movement and support its political program.[5] In the following community portraits, personal interviews, and discussions, I describe the variety of faith, politics, and lifestyles found in the Yesha communities.

JEWISH HEBRON: SACRED SITE AND BESIEGED TOWN

I began my visits and interviews in one of the most strident and militant settlements, the Jewish community in Hebron. Hebron is internationally famous as the site of the Tomb of the Patriarchs, the *Me'arat Hamachpelah*—known to Muslims as the *Haram al Ibrahimi*—where Jews and Muslims believe the progenitors of their religion are buried. Both communities come to pray there and both consider Hebron a sacred city. Since ancient times, Jews have had a close connection with Hebron. The Hebrew Bible records that the founding Hebrew patriarch, Abraham, settled in Hebron and purchased a family burial site there. The biblical Jewish King David, known as a great warrior who extended the boundaries of ancient Israel, was anointed king of Israel in Hebron. Throughout the millennia, excepting periods of war and expulsion, Jews have resided in Hebron. The "modern" Jewish community in Hebron begins in the sixteenth century, consisting of mystics who wanted to live close to the sacred environs of the Tomb of the Patriarchs. However,

Jews desiring to pray in the tomb had to remain outside on the steps leading to the entrance, as Islamic law defined the site as an exclusively Muslim religious site. Still, given the high regard for the spirituality and historical importance of Hebron, Jews in the ensuing centuries moved to the city, building synagogues and establishing yeshiva academies that attracted students from around the globe. Relations between Jews and Muslims were relatively harmonious during much of the nineteenth and early twentieth centuries, until the infamous 1929 riots. Incited by the anti-Semitic mufti Amin el-Husseini of Jerusalem, Arab rioters swept over all of Palestine, then under British mandate, and spread to Hebron, where sixty-seven Jews were killed, many more were injured, and some bodies were severely mutilated. Jews fled from Hebron after the 1929 riots, but though the long residence of Jews ended, the connection to and memories of the sacred city continued.[6] After the 1948–1949 wars, Hebron became part of the Hashemite Kingdom of Jordan and Hebron was Judenrein, without any Jews.

Historical events do not follow a direct path, and during the 1967 Six-Day War, Israeli forces making their way into the West Bank occupied the city and controlled it for the first time in two thousand years. The Tomb of the Patriarchs was open to Jews for the first time in centuries, and even secular Israelis saw the return to Hebron as a rendezvous with history finally making a loss right. In 1968, as discussed in chapter 1, a group of about seventy religious Zionist Gush Emmunim activists petitioned to spend the Passover holiday at the Park Hotel in Hebron. Israeli authorities were ambivalent about this incursion into an all-Arab city, but finally religious and historical memory triumphed, permission was given, and the "settlers" were later joined by scores of others who never left. Gradually, the community grew and attracted hard-core ideological settlers who established schools and rehabilitated old Jewish houses and synagogues, and Hebron became an important tourist center for religious Zionists. Currently—though these statistics are never exact and often the subject of political and diplomatic controversy—there are about two hundred thousand Palestinian residents and about five hundred to seven hundred Jews living in the city. The two communities live in the same city but are separated from each other, with little contact other than occasional confrontations. The bulk of the city is Palestinian and under the Palestinian Authority, with the Jewish settlers living in separate enclaves under Israeli military protection with guard posts and armored vehicles surrounding the Jewish enclaves. Hebron Arabs are known for their Islamic orthodoxy and are fiercely opposed to the Israeli presence, and street fights and attacks between settlers and locals are not unusual. Hebron Jews are known for their militancy, piety, and determination, and the community has been subject to ongoing terrorist attacks, located as they are amid a large militant Palestinian community. Almost every adult resident has a story of being attacked with thrown stones while driving. Some have experienced house invasions in which family members were killed, and others told me of sniper attacks while walking in the Jewish quarter. Hebron, unlike most other settlements, has no real local industry, farming, or business. Many of the residents are rabbis or teachers or are involved in publicity and tourism. In many ways, contemporary Jewish Hebron by its very existence is a testament to Jewish will and determination, and the simple act of residing there is the occupation of many of its residents. Much of the community's facilities—schools, playgrounds, housing development, synagogues, and recreation centers—are funded by an international foundation dedicated to supporting the Jewish presence in this historic place.[7]

BARUCH MARZEL: DEFENDER OF THE LAND

I traveled to Hebron to meet with and interview Baruch Marzel, a resident and well-known right-wing politician considered by many to be the spokesperson for extreme religious Zionist nationalism. Marzel had run for the Knesset in the 2013 elections on the ultranationalist Otzma L'Yisrael party line, but the party did not reach the minimum election threshold and no one from the party was seated. Marzel, who is an ordained rabbi and an attorney, is known throughout Israel as the uncompromising proponent for a Jewish state governed by religious Halachic law. He is a deeply committed social conservative opposed to feminism, a champion of large families, and opposed to homosexual rights—he is present at every gay pride parade, demonstrating against gay rights. He proudly told me that a woman's place was only in the home. He is a fierce nationalist and religious fundamentalist and absolutely and totally opposed to any type of territorial exchange. He has been arrested many times for civil disobedience and unlawful behavior in his campaign to stop the ceding of any West Bank lands, but he has a reputation for honesty and consistency even among his detractors. Marzel is considered extreme even by Hebron standards, but his views articulate central settlement concerns and goals.

I took an early morning bus from Jerusalem and was dropped off at the last stop at the foot of the Tomb of the Patriarchs. It was still early, and I asked the bus driver how to get to Tel Rumeida, the Jewish enclave where Marzel lived. The bus driver, surprised I was going there alone and unarmed, told me to go right up the hill but to be careful, as it is not a safe area for tourists or Israelis. I walked up the roadway among dozens of local Palestinians who were heading to work and going shopping but could not find the Jewish area. I did not think it a good idea to ask a local where Marzel lived and felt confused, anxious, and lost. I continued walking and shortly met a young Jewish settler with an Uzi and a pistol displayed prominently, who, seeing my confusion, offered to take me to Tel Rumeida. "Don't be afraid," he said to me; "in America you don't need weapons, but here we have to be prepared." He acted really tough, and frankly I was reassured to be in his presence because it did feel like a hostile environment for someone wearing an Orthodox head covering, as I did on the way to my interview. He accompanied me all the way to Marzel's house and, saying good-bye, gently castigated me for living in America. "Jews," he said, "ought to live in their own land."

Marzel resided not in a regular house but in a prefabricated "caravan," something looking like an old wooden railway car. His house was located on a hilltop surrounded by local Palestinian houses. The caravan had all sorts of bullet holes, which Marzel later explained came from shots fired from the surrounding Arab section of Hebron. Marzel, a bearded middle-aged man with a large kipah and a friendly demeanor, welcomed me into his home and ushered me into a sparsely furnished living room and dining room. "Ask anything you want," he said. "I speak frankly, not like many of our Israeli politicians." Marzel told me he was born in Boston, Massachusetts, and came to Israel as a young child. He became a devoted follower of Rabbi Meir Kahane, whom he always referred to as the "Rav," his rabbi and teacher. Rabbi Kahane was an American, the founder of the American Jewish Defense League, who urged Jews to take up arms in fighting anti-Semitism. Kahane immigrated to Israel, where he headed the ultranationalist Kach party, which had a strong following among right-wing nationalist and Sephardic Jews. Kahane was elected to the Knesset and had considerable popular support, but the Israeli political establishment, including the right-wing parties, viewed him as a racist for championing a controversial transfer program where Israeli Arabs would be forcibly transferred to surrounding Arab countries in what he viewed as a legitimate population exchange for those Jews from Arab lands who were forced to come to the new state of Israel in 1948. Kahane was radically anti-Arab—he saw Israel as a place only for Jews—and saw violence in defense of Jewish interests as necessary and desirable. Kahane maintained that it was Jewish passivity and the unwillingness to take up arms against their enemies that made the Holocaust possible. Kahane had a following in the United States, and his radical politics became increasingly popular in Israel after he took up residence there. The Knesset, however, outlawed his Kach party as violating the norms and laws of Israeli democracy and ejected him from the legislature. Kahane continued his political activism, speaking all over the world. On one of his trips back to the United States, he was murdered on November 5, 1990, in New York City as he was giving a speech to his followers. His assassin was El Sayyid Nosair, who was a follower of the radical Sheik Abdul Rahman, who ordered the first World Trade Center bombing in 1993. Marzel was an important figure in the Kach party, was the leading aide to Kahane, and headed Kahane's Knesset office during his tenure. After Kahane's death, he became and still remains the leading interpreter of Kahane's philosophy and political program.

Knowing this, I asked Marzel, "What would you do if today you were Israel's prime minister?" He responded readily, "I would tell the truth; the whole Land of Israel is ours; God gave it to the Jewish people. There is no possibility of compromise, and all this talk about peace with the Palestinians is nonsense." I interjected, but is it not a Torah injunction to protect human lives and would not giving up the idea of a greater Israel bring increased security for Israelis? Marzel considered me naïve and asked, "Don't you know what happened in Gush Katif?" Marzel was referring to the Israeli unilateral pullout from Gaza in 2005 and the forced removal of thousands of Israeli settlers and the destruction of some dozen communities with factories, hothouses, schools, and synagogues all demolished. The Israeli political hope at the time was that removal of the settlers and ceding the land to the Palestinians would reduce terrorist attacks on Israelis and encourage compromise and pave the way for a peace agreement. Not only did this not happen, he claimed, but under Palestinian control, terrorist factions became increasingly emboldened and rocket and mortar attacks were unleashed on Israeli cities.[8] The displaced setters who resisted eviction were never fully compensated and never able to reconstitute their community life. The result was serious civil and political conflict with no real gain. Marzel, as one of the militant leaders against the evacuation, asked me directly, "Tell me, did giving up Gush Katif bring tranquility? This is a delusion of the Israeli left and the Western countries who believe that a peaceful settlement is now possible. Are the regular attacks on our cities a sign of peace?" Marzel was insistent that any territorial compromise was forbidden by religious law and made no political sense, and that Israel's willingness to compromise was a result of the Jewish diaspora experience, which led to group insecurity and fearfulness. "It will take another generation of living in the land, but people will come around to my point of view. Over time, Rabbi Kahane's views will be acknowledged."

"What about the Arabs living as citizens within the 1948 borders?" I asked. "Would you transfer them as well?"

"The best thing is to help them leave, and with financial help, many do leave," Marzel said. He told me that there are ongoing covert operations encouraging Arab migration to Europe and America, offering financial incentives to those willing to leave. (This turned out to be true. Several informants close to the Israeli Foreign Ministry told me that the government was not opposed to this program.)

"What about those who do not want to leave?" I asked.

"If they stay and follow our rules and truly accept Jewish sovereignty, that's okay." I did not press Marzel on this point, though I knew of his views that the Arabs were the eternal enemies of the Jewish state and that any type of coexistence was illusion.

Marzel and his followers are known to have a confrontational style with the Palestinians, leading to numerous demonstrations in Palestinian communities and towns and often resulting in physical conflict with Palestinians. These acts, he explained, were necessary in order to demonstrate Jewish power and sovereignty. I tried to point out that all his confrontations and demonstrations only resulted in greater enmity between Jews and Arabs and did not change the political situation. Marzel was determined in his response. "I am not a politician," he said. "Someone must stand up for the full truth and really say what we must do even if it is currently unpopular." Here Marzel lashed out at the official Yesha leadership. "They know I am right, but they want acceptance by the media, by the academic elite, by the public, so they lie and pretend. I am the one who is honest because I want to speak the truth of our goals and not pretend and seek popularity. I do not trust Netanyahu at all. Some of the Yesha leaders may not like me, but many know that I am right in my positions. But they are afraid to support me." Marzel and his followers see the Yesha leadership as weak and unduly open to compromise with the government, too ready to give in to legal retractions and too accepting of government restrictions on settlement expansion. Marzel views settlement activity and Jewish law as superseding the Israeli legal system and Knesset legislation. He sees himself as the conscience of the Yesha movement, calling on them to uphold their religious and messianic goals.

I asked Marzel about the rise of so-called price tag violence, in which groups of civilian settlers retaliate against Palestinian attacks, burning Palestinian property and sometimes engaging in violent incursions. "There is a democratic state of Israel," I said. "So why not let the state authorities take care of this?"

Marzel was determined to explain the validity of these civilian attacks, which he saw as acts of self-defense. "We have a timid government afraid of international repercussions, and this passivity only unleashes additional attacks," he explained. Marzel pointed out that those communities that responded with a "price tag" action, such as Yitzhar in Samaria and Hebron, had relatively few attacks on the community and the residents there lived in relative security. "The Arabs around Hebron and Yitzhar know we can defend ourselves, and this actually stops violence," explained Marzel. He told me about the violence against Jewish civilians in Jerusalem, a mixed city with a large Arab population, where he felt the government looked the other way. This government refusal to act forcefully against Arab militants only encouraged continued attacks. I had heard similar views in other settler communities, where ordinary residents would bemoan the situation and say outsiders simply did not understand the intensity of violence and Islamic militancy and the absolute necessity, in their view, of a reciprocal defense. Vigilante violence, explained Marzel, is necessary in the current condition of government timidity.

I knew Marzel had demonstrated at Israeli gay rights parades, was absolutely opposed to marriage between Jews and Gentiles, and took issue with contemporary notions of sexual equality. I asked him about individual rights and personal autonomy, the hallmarks of Western democracy, in the society he envisioned for Israel. Marzel, himself the father of nine children, told me directly, "Women should stay at home and have babies." Democracy is fine, but a Jewish state has to insist on adherence to Halacha, he insisted. He told me that he personally got along with secular Israelis—and others have confirmed this—but Jewish law had to be followed in all areas of life in his conception of a Jewish state. Abortion and intermarriage had to be outlawed, and Torah law had to be followed. "What can I do?" he asked when I protested that this would deeply challenge individual rights, so much a part of the democratic ethos of the larger Israeli culture. "If the Torah decrees, I must follow and demand conformity." Here, I thought, was the crux of the issue, the clash between revealed truth not to be questioned or disputed and the culture of modernity, with its emphasis on individual rights, tolerance, and secular rationality. As I was leaving, I confronted Marzel about his rigid orthodoxy. I asked him to explain why Haredi anti-Zionist Jews who are similarly literalist and rigidly Orthodox oppose the settlement agenda and do not see the state of Israel as a harbinger of messianic transformation. His answer surprised me. "You are taken in by the media," he said. In fact, he claimed, Haredi Jews visit Hebron regularly, and many spend the Shabbat and holidays in the environs of Hebron. Many secular Jews visit as well, he explained, and are moved by the pioneering spirit and dedication of the Hebron residents. Indeed, this turned out to be true and shows a latent but significant level of support for the settlement enterprise. It turns out that sacred history and biblical narrative remain potent in the twenty-first century.

REFLECTIONS AND A TOUR OF HEBRON

I left Marzel's caravan feeling uncomfortable. He is a nice man, hospitable, with his home open to visitors and young Israeli soldiers who stopped in to have a snack. His house on the Sabbath is open to many visitors who do not necessarily agree with him, and it turns out he is always willing to dialogue and, though he is condemned by the Israeli media as a fanatic extremist, appears regularly on Israeli TV and is knowledgeable on social and cultural issues. I did not like what I took to be his fundamentalist social views, nor his support of vigilante violence, but some of his political interpretations had merit and were accurate. The unilateral Gaza pullout supported by the Israeli political establishment did not lead to better relations with the Palestinians but to the rise of militant Islam in Gaza and attacks on Israeli communities—and of course to the 2014 Gaza War, which occurred after I had met with Marzel and in some ways he had predicted. Marzel spoke of being honest and forthright in the interview, and I think he was. His views on Jewish sovereignty in the whole Land of Israel, on Israeli Arabs, on religion and state, and on the legitimacy of retaliation were very much the views of the settler movement, even if some leaders would not be as forthright about their agenda.

After I left Marzel, I joined a tour of Jewish Hebron with a group of visiting American Jews who had come to the city in an armored convoy. The tour was given by a Hebron resident, Rabbi Simcha Hochbaum, originally from the United States, who now worked as a tour guide and publicist for the settlement. Hochbaum gave an emotional talk about the importance of Hebron in Jewish history, the dedication of the current residents, and the dangers and violence they face from incessant attacks by Palestinian terrorists. We were shown houses where children and in one case several members of one family were killed, some gunned down on the road and others, we were told, killed during the Sabbath meal by armed attackers. Hochbaum explained that those killed were martyrs, Kedushim, holy ones who in their death were bringing messianic redemption. It is religious faith, he said, that sustains them, and they do have faith that their residence in Hebron is critical to ushering in the messianic age.

We were shown a beautiful nursery and kindergarten with dozens of little children playing and a reconstructed old synagogue. The community has dozens of young families, and despite the tensions and the presence of armed Israeli soldiers, the children looked happy and were having a good time. We saw schools and visited a restaurant and a book store and were shown the ancient hills where Jews had lived for centuries. Things looked normal, almost bucolic, but we were in a war zone. Rocks had been thrown at tour buses, and I witnessed some skirmishes between settlers and Palestinians. Still, to Hochbaum and the residents, Jewish Hebron was a dream come true.

We all stopped for a short memorial in several places where settlers had been gunned down in terrorist attacks. These were intense experiences, and the visitors were visibly moved by the stories of terror, especially by the harrowing tale of the murder of an infant girl, Shalhevet Pass, by marauders who had come on one Shabbat eve to kill at random.[9] The final stop on the tour was the old cemetery where the victims of the 1929 massacre were buried. Rabbi Hochbaum explained that the victims were mostly innocent yeshiva students—some of them American—who had come to study at this famed seminary located in the holy city. They were killed, he cried out, because they were Jews, murdered just like the millions of European Jews who were gassed in the ovens of the Holocaust for no other reason than that they were Jews. "We are now in our own state of Israel," he told the American visitors, and "we will never allow this to occur again." Hochstein told the visitors that the settlers represented a new Jewish consciousness: no longer will Jews be innocent victims and not fight back. Hebron shows that Jews can live anywhere in the Land of Israel, and no foreign nation can stop Jewish settlement. The Jews must now establish sovereignty over the whole of the biblical Holy Land.

We were all silent as a memorial prayer was recited for the victims from almost a century ago. Many of the visitors, most of whom were Orthodox Jews, were moved to tears, and some were so emotionally overcome that they had to be helped back to the tour bus. Here, I realized, was the deep attraction of many committed Jews to the Hebron community. They may not like their politics, but these American visitors identified with the settler situation; they too felt fear and anxiety over the Jewish condition as terrorism and violence against Jewish communities was breaking out all over the globe, but here were settler Jews who were standing up to attack and asserting their national sovereignty with courage and dignity. It occurred to me that bringing up Palestinian rights or ceding land to these visitors would not make sense. I wanted to ask these modern, educated American visitors what they thought of Marzel's politics, but I held back.

MA'ALE LEVONA: A VISIT WITH A YESHA RABBI

After seeing Hebron, I wanted to visit what to my mind is a more typical West Bank settlement, where people are not consumed by ideology and conflict but are ordinary Israeli citizens working and living in a suburban setting. The Ma'ale Levona settlement has a reputation as a moderate community with local industry and a variety of professional and high-tech residents, most of whom commute to work in Jerusalem, less than an hour's drive away. I particularly wanted to meet Rabbi Ari Weiss, [10] the official rabbi of the settlement. Weiss is a committed religious Zionist but is known for his moderate style and ability to connect with those outside the settlement world. I thought meeting him would give a different picture of the settlement enterprise.

Ma'ale Levona is situated in Samaria near the ancient site of the Shiloh tabernacle, which served as the first central ceremonial site in ancient Israel hundreds of years before the construction of the Temple in Jerusalem. The site of the Ma'ale Levona settlement was not random but was based on the historical and religious significance of the area. To religious Jews, this is sacred land, and the return of the Jews and the building of this settlement are not an incursion into foreign land but the fulfillment of biblical prophecy. The settlement is built on a mountaintop, from which one sees a panoramic view of the biblical Land of Israel. "Now you see why we are here," said Rabbi Weiss as he pointed out the historical sites. "There to the right is Shiloh, and look to the left and you can see the roadway that pilgrims took to make their way to Jerusalem for the festivals and to bring sacrifices." It was moving sitting in this biblical landscape, imagining pilgrims making their way to Jerusalem. We took in the beautiful view and then visited a neighboring house that has a traditional *mikveh*, ritual bath, carved in the ancient stones. The past and present seemed to be coming together in this setting. I saw the traditional mikveh, the ancient roadways; I was told of ancient pottery found at the site of the Shiloh temple, and I became confused. Things seemed so peaceful, and I felt as if I were in another time and place.

The landscape was indeed biblical, but the houses and the layout of the community looked to me like an American suburb, well kept, attractive, with nice gardens and single-family homes, and given the balmy weather, not unlike California. But this was not really the case. People drove to and from the community with weapons, and pistols were always at hand. After all, this is contested territory, and the bus I took to the community from the central Jerusalem bus station had bulletproof windows and steel shutters. Several of the passengers had rifles and a few armed soldiers were on the bus, reporting back to bases in the area. Despite my reverie, I knew that the area was the site of a number of serious terrorist attacks since its inception, and so I asked the rabbi, "What about the Arabs living in these territories and the Arabs living in the pre-1967 borders? How can there be peace and democracy in an exclusively Jewish state?"

Surprisingly, Rabbi Weiss quickly acknowledged the dilemma and freely agreed that the settlements were causing friction among Israeli Jews and were the reason for much international hostility toward Israel. "We do our share and God will do his share," was his response, and I was moved by his faith and his degree of religious modesty. This was something I often encountered among the mainline settlers, a fierce determination to settle the full Land of Israel, a faith that divine providence will see to it that they are successful, a sense that history is on their side, but recognition, however muted, that Jewish history is filled with setbacks. He continued: "Look what happened in the 1948 war, thousands of Arabs left their homes and abandoned their villages, and even now many Arabs want to leave this area." The religious believer, he explained, has *Emunah*, faith and conviction, which transcends political rationality and knows that God runs the world. "We know," he insisted, "that this is our place, the place of our forefathers, and if we settle the land, as is our obligation, and act justly, God will do his share and redemption will come."

As much as I respected his declaration of faith, I had to point out that former prime minister Ariel Sharon, once the leading architect of West Bank settlement, had been the mastermind for the unprecedented Gush Katif Israeli pullout, and the current right-wing prime minister, Benjamin Netanyahu, once an opponent of a two-state solution, now publicly advocated that territory in the West Bank would have to be ceded as part of a two-state solution. This appears to be a coming reality, I pointed out, and so I asked him, "What would you do if Ma'ale Levona had to be evacuated as part of an Israeli–Palestinian peace agreement?" Rabbi Weiss was forthright, though he responded Talmudically with a series of challenges. "What would you do if you were expelled from you home? What would anyone do? Would anyone not use any means to defend one's home? This is our home. What do you suspect; do we think we shall leave our home and not fight for our place?" Ultimately, despite his moderate tone, Rabbi Weiss agreed with Baruch Marzel. Israel was exclusively promised to the Jewish people, and the Palestinian people could enjoy local autonomy, but the state of Israel had to be an exclusively Jewish entity. Rabbi Weiss went on in this vein, and I felt he was annoyed with me for pursuing the line of questioning. Frankly, he thought me naïve and was disappointed that I did not fully understand the settlers' faith and predicament. "The world, including America, puts moral and political demands on us that they do not expect of themselves. Wait," he predicted, "what will happen in Europe in thirty years when, given the Muslim birth rate, 30 to 35 percent of Europeans will be Muslim. Do you think the Europeans will stand by to Muslim cultural invasion? No one wants their culture and their home taken over."

This was a theme of lament, disappointment, and anger I heard again and again from settler leaders and ordinary people. The Americans, they pointed out, can do as they wish. They can go into a foreign country, Pakistan, with an organized assault team and kill Osama bin Laden and some of his entourage, invade Iraq, intervene in civil wars all over the world, and when we, little Israel, want to defend our homeland from terrorists, the world is against us. America is applauded, the Israeli settlers point out, when it fights terrorism, but Israel is accused of violating international accords and censured by the international community when it targets known perpetrators of terrorism. The frequent labeling and stigmatizing of Israel as a warmonger, an aggressor, or a racist state intent on persecuting Palestinians is seen as wholly unwarranted by the settlers. They view their actions, as does the United States, as the defense of their rights and of the country. The settlers, and indeed many other Israelis, believe strongly that the international community is prejudiced against the Jewish state and that hatred and anti-Semitism motivate the outcry. Rabbi Weiss gave voice to this view when he talked about the European Holocaust. "Look," he insisted. "The Nazis started with the Jews and not one country in the international community came to our aid. In truth, most European countries were only too happy to get rid of the Jews. The Nazis began with the Jews but eventually all of Europe and America was engulfed in violence and terror. This is the situation today. Militant Islam targeting the Jewish state, but now the whole world is in danger from militant Islamic fundamentalists." The issue in the Middle East conflict, in Rabbi Weiss's view, is not Israeli settlement in the West Bank but the very idea of a Jewish state. It is Jew hatred, anti-Semitism, that fuels the conflict. "This is not a political dispute over territory," he explained, "but about Jewish existence as an independent people in their own nation-state."

I recalled as I was sitting on that beautiful mountaintop that this was the view of all the settlers I met. They were convinced that territorial compromise would not bring peace or change the standing of the Jewish state in the international community. Their view is that anti-Semitism and the world's desire to keep the Jewish people homeless and stateless are what drive anti-Israel sentiment. "Do you really believe we will have peace if the settlements disappeared?" The settlers again and again challenged me to recognize hatred of Jews. "Where is the fury against persecution of women in some Islamic countries?" they demanded. "What about the lack of personal freedom in Iran and the upheavals in Egypt?" The settlers, it turns out, see themselves as on the front line of a fight against totalitarian international militant Islam, bent, as they like to quote a former Islamic spokesperson, "on driving the Jews into the sea." The settlers maintain that the short-range Palestinian goal is to remove the Jews from Judea and Samaria, but the denial of Jewish sovereignty is the Palestinian endgame. Holocaust memories are deep, and just as the European world before World War II refused to recognize the totalitarian policy of Hitler, the international community today does not recognize the danger of militant Islam.

LUNCH AND A VISIT TO A WINERY

During lunch with Rabbi Weiss and his family, I learned that his wife was completing her PhD at an Israeli university, and she told me about a network of settlement women who were advocating for women's concerns. Again I realized how different these committed Orthodox Zionists were from their Haredi coreligionists. Although settlement women follow strict Halachic standards—hair coverings, long dresses—and sit separate from men at prayer and at public meetings, they hold some official settlement positions and their positions are articulated and often executed in key Yesha policies. The mayors of several important settlements are women, and women often lead settlement protest and advocacy groups. With few exceptions, all interviews and visits I had with settlement families included women, who were an integral part of the conversation and on occasion freely disagreed with their spouses. Lunch with the rabbi's family was no different. I had frequently pointed out to Rabbi Weiss the vigilante mentality among some of the younger settlers and that incidences of settler violence had to be held in check. The rabbi insisted I was overstating the case, and these few cases, as he put it, were the result of a handful of disturbed, wayward youth. I brought this up at lunch, and Mrs. Weiss immediately concurred with me and enumerated precise dates and places, challenging her husband's position and telling me her husband simply refused to recognize the severity of the situation. This occurred several times. Once, in Ofra, a particularly militant community near Jerusalem, an American man who had moved there was severely castigated by his wife for publicly taking what she thought was a pacifist position on retaliation, which she claimed was a defeatist attitude that would only lead to increased attacks. It dawned on me that the settler community was no traditionalist old-time community but a uniquely contemporary movement integrating religion, nationalism, and serious elements of modernity.

After lunch, Rabbi Weiss and I drove to the adjacent settlement of Shiloh, where we visited the town's winery and tasted some world-class wines. These are exported to the United States and Europe and are a source of considerable income and employment for the local community. I learned that several highly regarded wineries are located all over the West Bank, and the Bible and Talmud texts were scrutinized to discover the location of ancient sites for grape production. We were enjoying the wine and the beautiful scenery, and life seemed so peaceful and normal. Still, I insisted on asking the rabbi and the winemaker why so many Jews in Israel and abroad were so opposed to the settlement enterprise. Both explained—and I head this frequently from other settlers—that the opposition to the settlements lies in the vagaries of recent Jewish history. The nineteenth- and early-twentieth-century Zionist pioneers—the fathers of the modern state of Israel—were heavily influenced by European socialist and enlightenment ideals and came to Palestine to create a humanistic socialist utopia. Religion to them was something associated with the diaspora, with Jewish inferiority, with backwardness. The new Jewish settlements in Palestine were to be free of the constraints of religion, where Jews will live as normal people with a land of their own. Religion perhaps had a function to keep Jews united in a situation of statelessness, but with the return to normalcy it had outlived its usefulness and was contrary to the spirit of freedom and modernity. Religious setters challenge this secular Zionist view. To them, Israel is not a normal state but a sacred entity to bring redemption to the world, and to do this requires living a life based on religious observance and settling the whole Land of Israel. Rabbi Weiss maintained that most Israelis are actually supportive of the settlements, but the media and the academic and political elites want a fully secular society and their opposition to the settlements is deeply grounded in their antagonism to religious Judaism. They, the secular socialist Zionists, I was told, are envious of the settlers, their pioneering spirit, their patriotism, and their traditional families. Secular Zionism has outlived its usefulness, I was told, and ordinary Israelis are realizing that for Israel to survive religion must be part of an Israeli state and Israeli identity.

Much of our conversation was about politics, and before I left I asked a direct theological question to which I never received a direct answer from any settler: "Are we in the times of the Messiah spoken about in the Scriptures?" In good Jewish fashion, I was answered with a series of questions. "Look where you are sitting and drinking wine, look at the massive Aliyah of Jews to Israel, look at the flowering of the land, look at our high-tech accomplishments, and look at the growing return to religion. What do you think?" But, I asked, what about the restoration of the Temple, so much part of the messianic process? What about the messianic promises and agenda laid out in Jewish texts promising world peace? "That's a good question," I was told, "and time will tell all."

KEDUMIM: MAINSTREAM, MODERATE, AND IDEOLOGICAL

The large settlement town of Kedumim, spread over an area of three square miles with a population of about five thousand, is located in the hills of Samaria, not far from the Palestinian town of Nablus, on two adjoining mountaintops. The settlement, now an important and prominent center of the Yesha movement, began in 1974 with a Gush Emmunim group who sought to establish a settlement on the ruins of the Sebastia train station, dating from the Ottoman period. The initial settlement, as with so many others in the West Bank, was declared illegal by the Israeli government, and the early settlers were removed. The young Gush Emmunim activists persevered with sit-downs and illegal encampment, and finally permission was given for a small group to settle on the site of an army encampment in the area of Nablus. The settlement grew quickly and attracted young religious Zionists from all over Israel, soon becoming a major community in the West Bank.

Kedumim looks and feels like an upper-middle-class suburb, with many highly educated residents working in medicine, law, finance, and education. The community has several resident high schools and yeshivas and has some local industrial centers as well as agricultural business. The vast majority of the residents strongly identify with the *Dati leumi*, religious nationalist Zionist worldview, and are Orthodox in their lifestyle but open to secular education, arts, and music. The community has welcomed some nonobservant families as well, something not typical of Yesha settlements. I wanted to make a research stay in Kedumim because it seemed different from so many of the other West Bank communities. I had visited before and knew several long-term residents and leaders of the community, and while they were loyalists of the Yesha movement and firm believers in Jewish settlement, they were open and understanding of the complexities of Jewish settlement. The Kedumim settlers wanted settlement all over the biblical Land of Israel but appeared open to compromise and, unlike more militant settlers, appreciated Palestinian aspirations and resentments. Many of the people I knew and interviewed in Kedumim had a real sense of tragedy about the whole situation. The Palestinians had indeed lived in the land for centuries—this could not be denied—but Jewish history and the divine word also mattered. And there was the Bible and God's promises. The Jewish people had their mission, and this was not to be denied. The mood in Kedumim was very different from the militancy I encountered in Hebron.

A VISIT WITH A SETTLER FAMILY

I was hosted in Kedumim by the Gross family, who live in an attractive four-bedroom home that would not be out of place in a Los Angeles suburb. The Grosses have four children, all college educated. Three of the children are married with families living in Kedumim, and the youngest daughter was planning her wedding as I was visiting. Mr. Gross is a talented engineer, a graduate of the prestigious Haifa Technion who runs a successful international business developing and selling machinery used to purify wheat products for human consumption. Mrs. Gross is a science teacher in the local high school, and both have traveled throughout the world. They are modern and sophisticated, cosmopolitan people, knowledgeable about international politics, and so I asked them, "What made you come here to settle in a place much of the world calls 'occupied Palestine'?"

Their responses were not deeply ideological, nor did it involve much soul-searching or talk of God. "We were members of *Bnai Akivah,*" they said, a religious Zionist movement from which many of the Yesha leaders came, "and many of our friends encouraged us to join the new settlement so we could build the Jewish homeland. We were brought up in the movement, and this was an opportunity to realize our goals."

"What about the Palestinians, who claim this is their land?" I asked.

The Grosses were forthright in their response: "The land of Israel is a sacred place for Jews, and we must hold on to it." I was surprised by the matter-of-fact responses and the seeming lack of concern with the international consequences of Jewish settlement. But things were more subtle, and there was with the Grosses, as with many of the other Kedumim residents, a desire to find some solution to the issue, even if it did not entirely accord with their religious ideology. Beneath the trimmings of a comfortable middle-class situation, there was the fear of violence and attacks. Kedumim had a series of attacks and deaths of residents over the years, and there is among the residents the awareness that they were constantly living in a life-or-death situation. Many of the people I met in Kedumim were searching for a way out of the continuing violence and conflict.

Avigdor Gross spoke for many Yesha residents when he told me with resignation and sadness, "Look, there is nobody to talk with. The issue is not Kedumim or Shiloh in the West Bank. The Arabs do not want us here. They will never accept a Jewish state. They want Jerusalem and the whole country to be Muslim." And again the evacuation of the Israeli settlements in Gaza came up. "We left Gaza, and what did we get? Bombs falling on half of the country, and if, God forbid, we leave here in Samaria, the whole country, including Tel Aviv, will be under attack." Here was the Middle East tragedy; everyone was right and there seemed to be no way out. Gross was a practical man, a business-man, a Jew who felt he was a simple man and wanted to imagine a resolution to the century-old conflict, but none seemed imaginable.

AN "ILLEGAL" OUTPOST

After the Sabbath, Mr. Gross took me to a small "illegal" outpost—a tolerated but not governmentally approved village—called Havat Gilad, after Gilad Zar, who was a well-known chief of security for the Shomron settlement and was murdered in a terrorist attack in 2001.[11] Meyer Shimon, one of the founders of the community, explained that the settlement was established in honor Zar and that the goal of Yesha is to establish a new settlement whenever a settler is killed. This small com-munity of about twelve families is quite primitive. There are no houses, but each family has a "caravan," a small prefabricated trailer the size of an old railroad car. The Shimon family has four children, all living in two rooms. Shimon is employed as a lawyer at a Tel Aviv firm and moved in 2002 with friends and associates to the area to build the outpost, which only has intermittent electricity and is the target of Arab attacks. Mr. Shimon showed me several "caravans" that were burned in arson attacks by local Palestinian militants and told me about regular shootings and attacks on the residents as they were tending gardens and taking care of their children. Mr. Shimon is an unusually pious person, and he and his wife dressed in ultra-Orthodox Haredi fashion. He op-posed any violent response to the attacks on his settlement. I asked him why he insisted in living in such an insecure environment, in a settle-ment not even officially recognized by the Israeli government and close to hostile Arab villages. "Well," he said, "we are believers and pioneers building up the Land of Israel according to the Bible." He wife added, it's hard for Americans to understand, but "we are believers in Jewish destiny and in the words of the prophets. We do what God asked, and God will respond and bring the true redemption."

The Shimons are young, in their early thirties, and religious. They are opposed to any Israeli compromise with the Palestinians and distrusting of the official Yesha political leadership, whom they and others in radical outpost settlements see as having lost their pioneering spirit and been co-opted by the Israeli establishment. The Shimons were calm, patient, and cordial with my questions and challenges about international pressure, terrorism, morality, and the dangerous situation in which they and their young children were living. Essentially, they ignored the issues I brought up. They appeared confident and secure in their beliefs, pointing out that the community was growing and that Zionism means taking chances in order to secure a safe future for Jews in their homeland. Finally, after my continued prodding, Mrs. Shimon put it plainly to me: "You keep on bringing up the danger we live in. Were the Jews in Europe any safer than we are? Did you forget the Holocaust?" I had no response. The reality of anti-Jewishness is so recent and so enmeshed in Jewish history and consciousness that for these Jews, living in a dangerous environment but redeeming their sacred heritage is a sign of Jewish courage, continuity, and faith.

MEETING THE VICE MAYOR

I wanted to meet with the official Kedumim leadership, who are prominent in the larger Yesha movement and are known for their connections with the Israeli government. I arranged to visit the vice mayor of Kedumim, Raphaela Siegel, one of the original settlers and someone who has been a Yesha ambassador to Jewish communities in the United States. Raphaela Siegel is not a professional politician but an optometrist with a successful practice. She and her husband, a medical doctor, and their then five children moved to Kedumim, then a fledging settlement just being formed, in 1975 from cosmopolitan Tel Aviv. Raphaela liked city life, but as she put it, the Six-Day War was "the turning point in my life." It was not the victorious defeat of an enemy, she explained, but "the return of the sacred lands of Judea and Samaria to the Jewish people," which motivated her and her family to leave Tel Aviv and settle in the then primitive conditions of a new settlement, living in tents and caravans without paved roads and with intermittent electricity. "My husband and I felt that history, Jewish destiny, was calling us, and we moved from metropolitan Tel Aviv." They now live in a well-furnished and attractive house with several of their seven children in a desirable neighborhood in central Kedumim.

Raphaela began the interview in no uncertain terms. "Listen," she insisted, "this is the land God promised us, and this is the fulfillment of biblical prophecy." I pointed out that no one could deny that there were two peoples with two different religions and national identities living in the land. Both Jews and Muslims claim historical and religious rights to the land, and both have theological justification for their claims. Raphaela acknowledged this reality but honestly presented the Yesha view: "It's us or them. If, God forbid, a Palestinian state came about, it would be suicidal for Israel." Raphaela argued that, at this point in time, the Palestinian leadership was so fundamentalist and extreme and so supportive of terrorist attacks on civilians and bombings on Israeli cities that any talk of an agreement of any sort was illusory. In the Yesha view, she explained, there is no possibility of an agreement so long as the Palestinian leadership refuses to recognize the validity of a Jewish state in Palestine and continues to support terrorist attacks on the Israeli populace. The vice mayor claimed that the very time peace negotiations were going on with Israel, Palestinian TV stations encouraged attacks on Israeli civilians. She was adamant that despite Palestinian rejection of violence in international forums their leadership and Arabic media encourage violence and hatred of Israel, and in Palestinian schools, suicide bombers are glorified as heroes. "When a new generation of Palestinian leaders emerges who will renounce violence and recognize our rights to our historic homeland, then we can think about some sort of agreement."

This muted optimism intrigued me because this was the first practical talk of a possible rapprochement between the two parties I heard in conversations with Yesha people. I asked her to describe her view of a possible future resolution to the conflict. Here Raphaela presented what I came to understand is the moderate Yesha position. The West Bank lands referred to as Area C in the Oslo Accords,[12] where the majority of the Jewish settlements are located, "must remain as part of the Jewish Israeli state." Raphaela explained that this had to be the case because it would be impossible to remove thousands of Jewish residents in Judea and Samaria from their homes, settlements, and towns, where they had lived for almost half a century. In this Yesha plan—now supported by some current and former cabinet officials—Area C would immediately be annexed and become an integral part of Israel. Raphaela acknowledged that there are about fifty thousand Palestinian Arabs now living in that area, and these residents would be given the option to become full citizens of Israel with full legal and civil rights—something they do not currently enjoy—or continue to live in the area but align themselves with and be citizens of the adjoining state of Jordan. The other Palestinian areas in the West Bank would have local political autonomy—but not national sovereignty—and would be aligned with the Kingdom of Jordan, which already has a substantial Palestinian population. In this Yesha scenario, there would be no Palestinian state but Palestinian local autonomy in areas of the West Bank, always with an Israeli military presence on the land and in the air. I immediately countered that no Palestinian group, no matter how moderate or secular, would agree to such an Israeli-engineered arrangement. "Well, we must protect our rights to the Holy Land; any other setup is a recipe for national disaster," was Raphaela's immediate response.

IS RECONCILIATION POSSIBLE?

I thought at first that this response was simplistic and dismissive of Palestinian rights, but as I perused Palestinian Authority websites, it was apparent that some settlers' concerns were legitimate. Jews are described in these Palestinian publications as "barbaric monkeys" and "wretched pigs." Maps used in Palestinian schools and on Palestinian Authority publications do not show Israel but show the entire area as Palestine. Suicide bombers are portrayed as martyrs and heroes of the Palestinian people, and children are encouraged to emulate their suicidal actions. Militants convicted of attacks on Israeli civilians and subsequently freed in prisoner exchanges are welcomed as nationalist heroes and photographed in an embrace with the Palestinian president, Mahmoud Abbas. The settlers' intransigence was based on an accurate reading of the current Palestinian leadership.[13] Still, I was intrigued by the seeming simplicity of this Yesha peace plan as outlined by Raphaela Siegel. I thought it politically naïve and even illusory, and yet I wondered if her optimism, however impossible it appeared, was not at the heart of the entire Zionist enterprise. The early nineteenth- and twentieth-century Zionists were also seen as dreamers and rejected by much of the Jewish establishment. And yet within fifty years of the first formal Zionist congress, held in Basel, Switzerland, an independent state for Jews, the first in two thousand years, was declared in Tel Aviv. Perhaps Zionist dreams trump political realism. Perhaps the wild optimism and political "irrationality" of early Zionism accounted for the unpredictable Zionist successes. Perhaps Western rational politics cannot stop tribal nationalist visions, and in this way Yesha Zionist goals could be achieved.

Nonetheless, the plan for Palestinian autonomy as articulated by the Kedumim leadership ignored the reality on the ground and the serious historical and religious issues in the conflict between Jews and Muslims. The Palestinians have their own legitimate religious claims and have been living in the area for centuries. Their sense of loss and religious disappointment is enormous and appears to find no place in Yesha considerations. The settlers offer charity. To the Palestinians and to faithful Muslims all over the globe, the Holy Land is Dar al-Islam, the house and possession of Muslims, and can never be ceded to non-Muslims. I did not see how this Yesha plan could be reconciled with Palestinian aspirations and history. I voiced these concerns, which are shared by important elements of the Israeli political and intellectual elite, many of whom call for a complete separation between a Jewish Israel and a Palestinian state. Raphaela was adamant, insisting that no realistic and lasting peace could be had with an independent Palestinian state. I pointed out that the right-wing Netanyahu government itself was in favor of a two-state solution, and by all accounts this arrangement is the one favored by the United States and Europeans. "What would you do in the event the Israeli government goes along with the expected two-state solutions?" I asked.

I was surprised by her response. "We will have to go along with it peacefully. Never will we respond violently against the established democratic government. We will be sad, but we will have to accept the majority decision," she said. Finally, she added, "The messiah comes in small steps." For Raphaela, as for the other moderate, middle-class educated settlers, there is an inner struggle between theological beliefs and political reality. This contrasts with the views and politics of radical settlers living in Hebron, Yitzhar, and illegal outposts scattered throughout the West Bank, for whom there can be no talk of compromise. For them, holding on to the sacred soil is a holy war, even if this means civil disobedience and violent confrontations with other Jews. For the religious radicals, violence is on the agenda. In the suburban environs of Kedumim, political reality, it appears, would triumph over theological faith.

A view similar to Raphaela Siegel's scenario for a peace was taken by Dani Dayan, the former chairman of the Yesha Council, which represents some 350,000 settlers in about 150 West Bank settlements. Dayan is an iconoclastic but respected figure in the settlement world. He is not Orthodox but shares deeply the ideological view of Jewish settlement in the whole of the Land of Israel. His arguments avoid messianic or religious imagery but still emphasize the unique connection of the Jewish people to the West Bank. "If Israel detaches itself," he maintains, "from Hebron and Beth El and Shiloh, it will become an empty society, a shallow society that ultimately will forget why it's here." Dayan claims that those advocating a two-state solution are "either naïve or liars" because in his view both Jews and Palestinians have a claim on the entire area in question. Dayan's plan is to keep things as they are for the next decades, permitting the expansion of settlements and encouraging economic improvement for both Jewish and Palestinian communities. As things improve and the two communities learn to accept and tolerate each other, a unique arrangement will take place that will allow both peoples to share the area, with Jews living under Israeli sovereignty and Palestinians forming a political union with the Kingdom of Jordan. Dayan acknowledges the uniqueness and even abnormality of this long-term goal but says the Middle East is unique and that only unusual or unimagined arrangements will work. Dayan proudly points to several West Bank factories where settlers and Palestinians work together and to the Israeli Ariel University, located in the center of the contested West Bank but with Palestinians and Israelis studying together, as realistic examples of coexistence. Here, in the heart of the West Bank, is a well-regarded secular university where both peoples attend classes, obtain degrees, and interact in mutually beneficial ways in pursuit of economic and social advancement. Dayan, a successful and pragmatic entrepreneur, is convinced that time and, in his words, "the good life" will enable the two peoples to make a peaceable arrangement.[14]

THE KAHANE LEGACY: RADICAL ZIONISM AND MILITANT TRANSFORMATION

There are some in the settlement community who are deeply opposed to the moderate position of compromise, cooperation, and nonviolence. These settler fundamentalists want a Jewish state and full Jewish sovereignty over all of Judea and Samaria and see intimidation, population transfer, and violence as legitimate means to secure Jewish control and authority. These militant fundamentalists see the Israeli government as weak and view the official Yesha leadership as too willing to compromise with the Palestinians in order to secure an agreement to end hostilities. The militants want an immediate annexation of all of the West Bank, thereby establishing full and sole Jewish authority over the area. An American-born rabbi, Meir Kahane—who inspired Baruch Marzel—inspires much of the settler militancy. Kahane was never an important figure in the settler leadership and was considered an outsider. Still, his militant ideology and his support of radical action influenced many. He was the founder of the militant American Jewish Defense League, which champions a combination of civil disobedience and vigilante violence to protect American Jews from anti-Semitic attacks. The American government eventually listed the Jewish Defense League as a domestic terrorist group, and Kahane allegedly emigrated to Israel to avoid an American prison term.

Kahane arrived in Israel in September 1971 and immediately established an Israel version of the JDL, which he called Kach, and preached and practiced his philosophy of Jewish might and the need for violence in defense of Jewish and Israeli interests. In Israel, the danger to the Jewish people, in Kahane's view, was the very presence of Arabs, whom Kahane saw as a fifth column, an internal political and religious threat. Kahane's solution was forced migration from Israel for all Arabs, albeit with compensation and agreements with surrounding Arab countries. His message of Jewish power and honor and his fierce justification of violence in defense of Jewish interests resonated with considerable numbers of poorer Jews from Muslim lands and with elements in the radical settler community. Kahane and his followers began a series of attacks and provocations against local Arabs in an attempt, in their view, to protect themselves and to show the Arab populace that Israel was an inhospitable place for them. Throughout the 1970s, 1980s, and beyond,

Kahane's followers, living in some of the radical settlements in Judea and Samaria, continued their intimidation and confrontational campaign for "transfer," their term for the movement of Palestinians to Arab countries. In the Kahanist view, negotiation, compromise, and a limited lawful response to the conflict with their Arab neighbors would never work. Jews had to stand up and be willing to kill and be killed in defense of their rights to their historic homeland. For Kahane and his followers, the Jewish avoidance of violent confrontation was the result of millennia of Jewish passivity and statelessness, which in its own way made Jews easy prey to anti-Semitism. Jews, argued Kahane, needed to be tough and show their adversaries that they could be as aggressive, violent, and bloodthirsty as their enemies. Kahane, in a highly original way, linked his call for Jewish violence with the classical Jewish theological emphasis on *Kiddush Hashem*, sanctification of God's name, and *Hilul Hashem*, profaning of God's name. In his manifesto, *Listen World, Listen Jew*, he put it this way:

> A Jewish fist in the face of an astonished Gentile that has not seen it for two millennia, this is Kiddush Hashem. Jewish domination over the Christian holy places while the Church that has sucked our blood vomits its rage and frustration. This is Kiddush Hashem.
>
> Do you want to know how the name of God is desecrated in the eyes of the mocking and sneering nations? It is when the Jew is beaten, God is profaned! When the Jew is humiliated God is shamed. When the Jew is attacked it is an assault upon the name of God.[15]

After his emigration to Israel, Kahane identified all Arabs as the eternal enemies of the Jewish people who were out destroy the state of Israel and repeat the events of the European Holocaust. Jews had to use every means to protect themselves, and for Kahane and his followers, this meant expelling all Arabs from Israel and from Judea and Samaria. Removing all Arab Palestinians and making Israel a fully Jewish country would require Jews to stand up to the international community, be assertive, and declare their sole rights to the Land of Israel. Kahane saw the Israeli political and academic elites as his foes who wanted to curry favor with the international community and be seen as tolerant, democratic, and peace loving, putting the state of Israel and its Jewish population in mortal danger. He saw Arabs as the mortal enemy of the Jewish people "who curse, and stone and shoot and bomb Jews and vow to drink Jewish blood." To Kahane and his followers there could be no compromise, no tolerance of Arabs in the Israeli state. It was, in his view, a Jewish illusion that Jews and Arabs could live peaceably together. To be safe in their own land, Jews had to courageously declare that "Eretz Yisrael is ours and that the Arabs are our sworn enemy—sworn to destroy us, they attempted to do so often in the past. And then—*throw them out!*"[16]

Kahane was despised by the Israeli establishment, and he was never part of the settler leadership, who were suspicious of him as an American outsider and preacher of violence. Kahane did gather a small but faithful following in Israel, was eventually elected to the Israeli parliament, and had several West Bank communities organized following his radical agenda. In the 1980s, with his popularity on the rise, the parliament and the Supreme Court declared his party racist and illegal. Following his disqualification, Kahane became a somewhat marginal figure in Israeli politics but continued to speak and lobby for his program all over the world.

VIOLENCE IN THE NAME OF RELIGION

The tale of Kahane and his extremist agenda did not end there. His followers, including Dr. Michael Ben Ari and Baruch Marzel, have run in parliamentary elections (Ben Ari was elected and served and Marzel is on the ballot in the 2015 elections and as of this writing appears to have a good chance of being elected), and the Kahanist political program still has support among groups of radical settlers and many of the young radicals in the "illegal" outpost settlements. Among Kahane's earliest and most fervent supporters was Dr. Boruch Goldstein, an American emergency physician who immigrated to Israel and lived in a settlement community close to Hebron and the Tomb of the Patriarchs. Early on February 25, 1994, a Friday morning, Goldstein hid himself in the tomb and opened fire on Muslim worshippers, killing twenty-nine people and wounding scores of others. Goldstein's murderous rampage shocked the Israeli public, who could not imagine that a seemingly normal man, committed to his family, a distinguished physician, and by all accounts a mild-mannered person, had committed such an act. Yitzhak Rabin, then prime minister of Israel, pronounced Goldstein a "madman" and "insane." The Israeli media and political pundits all went along with this view, condemning the murders and expressing collective remorse and insisting that this was the act of a deranged killer.

The facts of Goldstein's life and motives did not easily support this view. Goldstein, until the attack, was a much sought-after physician who, by all accounts, had no history of violent behavior and had treated both Jewish and Arab patients. However, he had imbibed the Kahane philosophy of Hilul Hashem and Kiddush Hashem and saw the recent Oslo Accords as a sellout of Jewish rights and a terrible return of Jewish passivity and unwillingness to assert their ancestral rights to the biblical homeland. For Goldstein, the Palestinians had to learn that Jews and Israel are powerful and violent, and if the Israeli government would not stand up for Jewish honor and sovereignty, then martyrs had to offer their lives in support of Jewish destiny. In Goldstein's West Bank community, he was seen as a heroic figure, having been killed in his attempt to assert Jewish honor and power in a time of Israeli capitulation to Arab terror. A memorial site in Goldstein's settlement community of Kiryat Arba was erected adjacent to his gravesite, which became a religious shrine attracting sympathetic pilgrims from around the world. "This was the man," read a sign at the site, "who avenged Jewish blood."[17]

Militant messianism means that political reality must conform to religious ideology. This was precisely the case with twenty-five-year-old Yigal Amir, an Israeli army veteran and a brilliant law student at Bar-Ilan University who in November 1995 assassinated the then prime minister, Yitzhak Rabin, because Rabin had agreed to the Oslo Accords, which called for shared sovereignty with the Palestinians as a way to end the conflict. Israel was once again shocked by the violence against a war hero and a famed politician, but Amir was no deranged or lonely gunman. He was a recognized scholar of the Talmud and deeply committed to the settlement movement, though he himself was not a resident, and evidence showed that he had discussed the religious permissibility of assassinating Rabin with numerous friends, colleagues, and distinguished rabbis. Perhaps most surprising and frightening to the secular Israel populace was that Amir's transformative Zionist ideology was not idiosyncratic but shared by a not-insignificant number of religious Zionists all over the world. "God gave the land of Israel to the Jewish people," he explained to his interrogators, and he, Yigal Amir, was making certain that God's promises, which he believed in with all his heart and mind and to which he committed his life, were not denied. He could not stand by passively, he declared, while the Jewish state reneged on its birthright and abandoned the biblical homeland. In his religious understanding, Amir explained, his act was not the result of an emotional response but a way of making things right. It was an action dictated by the Torah to impede a religious and national catastrophe, which would have taken place under the leadership of Yitzhak Rabin.

According to Amir, Rabin deserved to die because in agreeing to cooperate with the Palestinian authorities he was facilitating the possible mass murder of Jews by Palestinian militants. This gave Rabin, according to Halacha law, the status of *rodef*, a person about to kill an innocent person and therefore liable for execution by any bystander without trial. Rabin was also, he explained, a *moser*, a Jew who willingly betrays his brethren and was guilty of treason against the Jewish nation. In Jewish tradition, rodef and moser are among the most pernicious activities, and such people are to be killed. Most rabbis in the settlement camps disagreed with Amir's theological stance, but rabbis allied with the radical settlers had before the assassination expressed similar views, though they never outrightly called for Rabin's murder. "It is the obligation of the community leaders," they proclaimed, "to warn the head of the government and his ministers that if they keep pursuing the Oslo agreement, they will be subject to the halachic ruling of *din moser* as ones who surrender the life and property of Jews to Gentiles."[18] Amir did not innovate or fabricate his argument for the assassination of Rabin, but rather was continuing a religious view of the sacred rights of Jews to the whole of the Land of Israel.

Perhaps the leading contemporary radical theologian justifying violence and celebrating the action of Goldstein is Rabbi Yitzchak Ginsburg, an American-educated mathematician who is known as a leading cabalist and the head of the radical yeshiva Od Yoseh Chai, now located in the militant Yitzhar settlement. Ginsburg does not live in any of the settlements in Judea and Samaria and is viewed with suspicion by the mainstream settler leadership and populace, with whom he is often in religious and political disagreement. He is seen as someone who incites insurrection against the government and provides theological encouragement for violence against Arabs. Ginsburg's best-known work is his monograph *Boruch Hagever*, literally, "Blessed Is the Man," which is a theological justification for Goldstein's rampage. The key element in Ginsburg's theology is the ontological distinction between Jews and non-Jews. In Ginsburg's theology, Jews are created in the image of God and have special merit and standing in the divine plan, and given this special standing, any harm or threat to Jewish honor or life calls for reprisal and revenge, including murder, which according to Ginsburg is justified by Halacha. In Ginsburg's teachings, the life of a Gentile is inferior to that of a Jew, and even the perceived threat of Arab violence against Jewish settlers justified Goldstein's murderous rampage. In a section decrying the Israeli public's shame and revulsion, Ginsburg argues that Goldstein's motives were religious and pure, based on the rational calculations of a learned Talmudic scholar and physician and not on personal hatred or animosity. His motives, Ginsburg writes, "were fully Jewish acting for pure and justified revenge."[19]

Ginsburg echoes Kahane's view of violence as Kiddush Hashem, a glorification of God, and as an obligation to protect Jewish standing and honor, for any insult to Jews is an act against divine honor. He sees religious value in Goldstein's actions as a martyr's act of self-sacrifice to protect Jews from Arab attacks. Ginsburg, as a talented cabalist, goes further; he sees Jewish violence and martyrdom as appeals to God to protect his chosen people. The willingness to seek revenge to the point of murder and violence, Ginsburg explains, will cause heaven to respond to Jewish suffering and encourage divine help to be shown. In this worldview, violence and martyrdom are not only political acts to be seen in worldly terms but have the power to encourage, perhaps force, divine redemption. In this cabalistic view, the Jewish martyr's blood must be avenged by the heavenly forces. Ginsburg's views are not those of most Modern or even Orthodox Jews, but he is correct in arguing that his views are supported by biblical, Talmudic, and cabalistic literature.

SACRED FURY: THE VOICE OF YOUNG RADICAL SETTLERS

The Yesha leadership is fully opposed to these radical views and sees vigilante violence as dangerous, immoral, and counterproductive to molding a national consensus for settlements in Judea and Samaria. Nonetheless, vigilante cells are growing in many radical settler communities. I was most interested to talk with some of these radical activists, and I arranged to visit and interview groups of radical settlers living in the communities of Kiryat Arba, Kfar Tapuach, and Yitzhar, all of whom are inspired by the teachings of Rabbis Kahane and Ginsburg.[20] They were largely young, very religious, many with long earlocks and wearing the large *tzizit*, fringe garments, associated with the ultra-Orthodox non-Zionist Haredim. They were surprisingly friendly and straightforward about their religious ideology, politics, and price tag activities. They see themselves as religious patriots, as nationalists who are defending their homes and standing up for Jewish rights. They see the Israeli government as politically weak, intimidated by international pressure, and unwilling to protect the settlement communities from terrorist attacks on West bank roads, stone throwing, and murderous home break-ins that have killed scores of setter families, including the violent murder of small children and even of infants. Their fury at the government, including the right-wing Likud party led by Prime Minister Netanyahu, I discovered, is fueled by their view that the government and the Israeli military leadership have lost their strong identity with Jewish history and have abandoned confidence in Jewish divine rights to the Land of Israel. Over and over, I heard comments defending their reprisals and political positions, sometimes almost said beseechingly: "We are the real pioneers, we are the real Zionists, and we are doing just what the first and second Aliyah people did, settling the land and defending it, making it a Jewish homeland, but we are pilloried, insulted, and called Jewish terrorists." The anger and disappointment among the radical young settlers extend to the Yesha rabbinical leadership, who have condemned their activities as prohibited by Jewish law. I was surprised at their lack of faith in the teachings of the settler rabbinical leadership.

One young man, Ben Meir, living in a small outpost outside the Samarian settlement of Bet El, known to be the home of many hard-liners and led by Rabbi Eliezer Melamed, known for his scholarly writing in support of Yesha, explained to me that the rabbis could not be trusted to lead the settlers. "Look at what happened in Gush Katif," he explained, referring to the 2005 Israeli pullout from Gaza. Thousands of settlers were uprooted from their homes—some remained homeless for a long time—synagogues were destroyed, and factories and profitable hothouses were closed in an unsuccessful attempt to broker a peace agreement. Additionally, Hamas militants used the liberated Gaza as a base to launch rockets over much of Israel. Ben Meir was upset with the government, but his anger and seething disappointment were mostly directed at the Yesha rabbis. "They said it will never happen, the government will not be able to evict the Jews in Gaza, and surely God will stop it at the last moment," he remembered. Ben Meir and his peers felt they were on their own and that what they were doing was just and legitimate to defend themselves. Many were young teenagers when the Gaza evacuation took place, and they were encouraged by the rabbis to believe that the Gaza communities would never be destroyed. Here was a growing generation gap. The senior leadership and the first generation of settlers were particularly responsive to the Halachic rulings and ideological direction of Yesha rabbis. The young radicals, socialized to have full faith in rabbinical authority, now rebel against what they see an erroneous and misguided leadership.

The militant settlers conduct what has been termed a "price tag" policy—*tag machir*—in which Palestinian attacks on Israeli settlers or property are answered with acts of retaliation, including random violence against Palestinian communities. Such acts include burning Palestinian property, uprooting olive trees, arson, burning mosques, and mass demonstrations blocking roads. The price tag tactics are aimed at Palestinian militants but increasingly have the goal of challenging the Israel government and wreaking havoc on the Israeli military administration in the West Bank. One settler explained that roadblocks and tire burnings are set up whenever the Israeli government seeks to demolish an "illegal" outpost. Some radical setter groups have gone so far as to call for the stoning of Israeli soldiers when they attempt to evacuate a new unauthorized outpost. The price tag activists are small in number—estimates range from several hundred to several thousand participants—but they are an important element in the settler world. In many ways, these radicals give voice to the resentment settlers and their sympathizes harbor against the government.[21]

The government and the full political spectrum, from left to extreme right, have denounced the price tag policy as immoral and detrimental to Israeli society and Israel's international standing. Voices from the secular establishment are particularly strong in their denunciation. The internationally known author Amos Oz called the young Yesha radical groups "Hebrew neo-Nazis," an especially derogatory term in the Israeli context.[22] The Yesha settler leadership as well, including some of the militant leaders, have denounced these acts, and one Yesha leader, Elyakim Haetzni, a famed lawyer and right-wing activist, called them "despicable." Yesha rabbis, including the most radical Yesha theologians, have joined in condemning price tag acts and retaliation, including Rabbi Zalman Melamed, who called upon his congregants not to engage in any attacks on Palestinians. Rabbi Ari Weiss of Ma'ale Levona told me all Yesha rabbis ruled that vigilante violence, even after terrorist attacks on settlements, is wrong, and he and other rabbis explain that defense and retaliation are the responsibility of the government alone.

These public declarations are sincere, but the residents in Judea and Samaria live in fear of daily terrorist attacks and believe the government is not fully behind them and that the political and secular elites want nothing more than to abandon the settlement enterprise and retreat to safety in Tel Aviv and its environs. Most of the settlers, I believe, don't like their radical youth battling with the Israeli Army and police, nor do they desire random attacks on Palestinian civilians, and while they may not approve of the policy, they understand, appreciate, and sympathize with the frustration and anger. According to some surveys conducted among all Israelis, both settlers and those living within the Green Line, a considerable portion—one survey in 2011 found 40 percent—believe that price tag action, particularly after attacks on civilians, is "justified to some extent."[23] Such attacks on civilians are considered particularly pernicious by the Israeli public.

Sometimes an outside journalist catches the mood of a society best. In a challenge to those disapproving of the price tag retaliation, an Italian journalist, Giulio Meotti, wrote:

> Let's be honest and go straight to the point: those who obsessively focus on "price tag" would like to see the Jews of Judea and Samaria lie down and die. For them, the Jews, especially in Judea and Samaria, are the ones who should be victims. The doors of the ghetto have been drawn in Tel Aviv.
>
> If you live in the hundreds of outposts throughout the Biblical heartland, where the fear of being killed is palpable and the psychological impact on children and adults alike is immense, is it so un-

thinkable and unreasonable to show the Arabs some physical, non-injurious deterrence against terrorism?

In the Middle East, if you show weakness you will be treated as weak and will be taken advantage of at every opportunity. If you behave with strength and decisiveness, you will survive. True, the IDF [Israel Defense Force] should be the only one justified to use force to protect Israel's citizens, but what happens when you see the army retreating from protecting you and the Arabs reach the gates of your besieged community?[24]

It is this psychological condition to which, despite the official rabbinical and political leadership objection, the price tag policy speaks and why there is considerable sympathy and tacit approval to violent Jewish responses. Whoever travels or lives for a time in the territories sees and experiences the anxiety, fear, and unpredictability of everyday life. The sense of vulnerability, powerlessness, and danger is often masked by ideological platitudes and religious certainty, but the fear and anxiety are always there. The radical and sometimes violent youth have found a response to their precarious predicament. And it is to this reality that Rabbi Ginsburg speaks so powerfully. Feeling abandoned by the compromises of the official Yesha leadership, and disappointed by their Yesha rabbis, who assured them that the Gaza settlements would never be evacuated, but infused with the ethos of militant Zionism from childhood to settle the whole of the contested West Bank, the youths are justified by Ginsburg's kabbalistic and Talmudic justification of renegade violence, which provides religious legitimacy. In this view, based on Ginsburg's analysis of the Talmud's dictum, "If someone is about to kill you, kill him first" (Talmud, 72A), threats or danger to settlers justify defensive violence.[25]

Ginsburg is a radical thinker, and his positions, theological and political, are rejected by virtually all Israelis, including mainline members of Yesha. Still, his emphasis on Jewish honor and vulnerability resonates with many Israelis, not just the radicals who are his most fervent followers. In this regard, the events of past Jewish persecution and most prominently the European Holocaust have affected Jewish and Israeli psychology and self-understanding. Israelis see themselves as a beleaguered minority nation open to attacks by Islamic militants, fearful of annihilation and misunderstood and devalued by an international community still in the grip anti-Semitism, now camouflaged as anti-Zionism. Ginsburg is a voice on the periphery, but his assertion of the necessity of Jewish power and violent self-defense resonates with many Israelis. Ginsburg and his followers are rejected, but his articulation of Israeli and Jewish fears, anxieties, and vulnerabilities is recognized by his countrymen.

As I have discovered in my visits and interviews, there are many Yesha voices and positions. The popular journalistic view of the settlers as a monolithic, fanatical, violent movement is an exaggeration. Similarly, the view of the settler movement as a passing phase of extreme religious nationalism soon to return to a more balanced and "realistic" political Zionism is also incorrect. Yesha settlement theology and politics for the foreseeable future are here to stay, and in the concluding chapter I discuss the significance of militant Jewish religious nationalism for the future of Judaism, the Middle East, and world peace.

5

JUDAISM, RELIGIOUS NATIONALISM, AND THE MIDDLE EAST CONFLICT

LIVING IN THE HOLY LAND

Yesha religious Zionism is a rebellion against traditional Jewish culture and at the same time a faithful and legitimate continuation of Talmudic and rabbinical teachings. Since the Roman victories over the Jewish communities in the Land of Israel in the first and second centuries, rabbinical teaching has decreed that Jews were forbidden to use force to reclaim the Land of Israel and establish a Jewish national entity. Traditional Judaism claimed that messianic redemption and return to the homeland would occur, but only through a miraculous and solely divine event. In the meantime, the faithful Jew waits patiently, doing good deeds, meticulously following religious law, and praying and studying, with full faith that in God's time messianic redemption will come. The holiday liturgy enshrines this view, proclaiming, "But because of our sins, we have been exiled from our land and sent far from our soil,"[1] and beseeching divine intervention to end the dispersion and have the Temple rebuilt in all its majesty and glory.

However, alongside this view of Jewish sinfulness, inferiority, and passivity was the continuing belief in the chosenness of Israel, the special covenant between God and the Jewish people, and the continuing attachment to the ancient homeland. There was strong sentiment in the Talmudic, medieval, and early modern periods that Jews not take any organized political measures to settle or return en masse to the land of their forefathers, but the sacred writings continued to argue that a complete Jewish life cannot be realized in the diaspora, and the obligation to settle and establish Jewish sovereignty in the Land of Israel continued, if only in a theological and spiritual form. Put differently, there was considerable ambivalence in the Halachic tradition. Jews were concurrently obligated to claim their rights of settlement and national sovereignty, but due to Gentile hatred and political impotence, they were not to do anything to reclaim the land. They could go on spiritual pilgrimages and settle in small religious enclaves—as some did throughout the ages—but always as a pariah people, acknowledging their inferior status under the aegis of Gentile governments.

These practical restrictions and theological inhibitions did not dampen the Jewish connection with the Land of Israel. The scriptural passages bequeathing the homeland of the Jewish people and the assurances of world redemption and blessing that would come to all through the Jewish people were too strong to disregard. The Talmudic rabbis, for example, living in Babylonian communities outside the Land of Israel, maintained that the Jewish lunar calendar—upon which ritual observance is set—had to be set according to astronomical events as they occurred in the biblical Land of Israel. Authoritative medieval commentators, such as Nahmanides, ruled that the mitzvah commandment for Jews to conquer, settle, reside in, and populate the Land of Israel continues in every age. Nahmanides argued, moreover, that this Halachic obligation is religiously commanded according to biblical law. The towering medieval philosopher and Halachic authority Maimonides, often in theological disagreement with Nahmanides, did not rule that residence in the Land of Israel is necessarily a direct biblical mitzvah commandment, but he too saw Jewish residence as religiously obligatory. Rabbi Tzvi Yehuda Kook, the founding theologian of messianic Zionism, appropriated Nahmanides's theological formulations in the medieval *Sefer Hamitzvot* to justify Jewish settlement and conquest in Eretz Yisrael as a mitzvah obligation in every time and in every generation. It is true that Kook was writing as a twentieth-century messianic Zionist advocating settlement and armed conflict to secure the whole of the Land of Israel, but he was absolutely correct in seeing a direct line between himself and the Jewish classical rabbinical position. As he put it, "It is well known that the Ramban [Nahmanides] established a fundamental *Halachic* ruling that living in the Land of Israel and conquering the Land, are commandments in the Torah which apply in every age . . . possessing the Land is a mitzvah and the opposite is a rebellion."[2]

Not all rabbinical authorities concurred with Nahmanides. Still, from the medieval period through the modern age, there was wide and deep consensus in the Halachic writings on the religious obligation of Jewish settlement in the Land of Israel.[3] This normative Talmudic and rabbinical view on Jewish rights to the Land of Israel was never disputed. There were, through the ages, more positive rabbinical voices directly advocating Aliyah, emigration to the Holy Land; others supporting Aliyah but counseling greater restraint; and still other rabbinical voices, fearing an anti-Jewish backlash, advocating a more passive, even apocalyptic, response. But there was, at least until the beginnings of the modern Zionist movement, an acceptance that the Jewish return to Israel was difficult, and for most Jews impractical and impossible to fulfill. True, there were scriptural and rabbinical imperatives to reclaim the land, but Jews simply did not have the political power and social will to realize this religious national goal. While the mitzvah obligation might not be possible, however, the goal was never to be abandoned. Religious faith meant that in time Jews would once again establish a national homeland in the biblical Land of Israel. This cardinal belief was central to traditional Jewish faith and illustrates the potency of historical and cultural memory.

RELIGION AND STATE: THE YESHA SYNTHESIS

Here again the charismatic Kook articulated the Yesha Zionist vision and its continuity with traditional theology:

> If during generations of Galut, we were in situations preventing us from keeping the precepts of settling and taking possession of the land of Israel due to the realities of Galut, both psychologically and practically, and because of the gentiles who established decrees in our Land who seized from us the possibility of keeping the most serious precept in its wholeness, behold, this does not alter the essential of the obligation of this precept and all its stringent requirements. The obligation to do a commandment isn't nullified because of a situation where one is prevented from doing it. In our genera-

tion, in which we merited to experience wonders of God and his righteous judgments in the complete crystallization of the end of Galut's revelation, the impediments fell away and the obstructions separating us from our land disappeared before us.[4]

In Kook's formulation, the momentous religious Zionist breakthrough makes messianic religious nationalism possible and in consonance with traditional Halachic theology and law. The obligation to conquer and settle the land was always to be fulfilled, and now, this mitzvah obligation can be enacted in the new conditions of statehood. To Kook and his disciples, these new conditions meant that the messianic process was directly unfolding and the state was the vehicle for messianic redemption. This was an enormous redefinition of Jewish religious faith, piety, and practice. Not the synagogue, not just Talmudic study, not meticulous observance of the minutiae of religious ritual alone, but the state, its institutions, its army, and the parliament were to be the handmaidens of messianic transformation. The formally secular was now holy and sacred. Zionism, in this view, was not merely a political nationalist movement to aid a homeless people but a religious nationalism with messianic goals. "It is through the Nation of Israel, in its national character in the Land of Israel, and in its statehood among the nations of the world, that the sanctification of Hashem's [God's] name appears. . . . The sanctification comes through the nation, the *Tzibur*, the congregation of Israel, which achieves its most complete expression in Statehood as we approach the messianic ideal."[5]

Not all religious Zionists went along with Kook's full messianic vision of the new state of Israel, but even his detractors agreed that reclaiming their ancient homeland and establishing an independent state represented elements of messianic fulfillment. The trauma of the European Holocaust and the sentiment that Jews had no safe haven among the nations of the world to gave great impetus to the religious Zionist vision. Now the mitzvah to settle the Land of Israel was not merely a spiritual goal to be carried out in a distant future, but a realistic and necessary goal to be implemented. The Israeli Declaration of Independence in 1948 was clearly a political victory for the Zionist movement, but for religious Zionists it was also a divine miracle and a sign of the messianic redemption foretold in the Jewish scared scriptures. Shortly after the establishment of the state of Israel, two hundred of the world's most prominent traditional Orthodox rabbis signed a proclamation stating,

"We thank Hashem [God] for granting us the privilege—with his abundant mercy and kindness—to witness the first flowering of the beginning of redemption through the establishment of the state of Israel."[6] This religious messianic fervor was shared by all traditional Jews, including those who had previously distanced themselves from the Zionist movement.[7]

The state of Israel, then, from its very beginning, was seen as a messianic and miraculous entity through which biblical prophecy was to be fulfilled. And it was not far to move from seeing the emergence of the state as a messianic event foretold in scripture to the Yesha position of full sovereignty and settlement in the whole of biblical Israel. As early as the 1950s, long before the 1967 Six-Day War and the Israeli acquisition of the West Bank, rabbinical proclamations were issued against relinquishing any part of the biblical homeland or signing political agreements that would partition the land.[8] The settlers did not initiate a novel view of the state of Israel but implemented an already extant rabbinical view of the messianic dimensions of the new state. Yesha messianic Zionism, then, is not a *novum* in Jewish theological thinking or Halachic decision making but a continuation, refinement, and reinterpretation of traditional jurisprudence. The Yesha theology is, in many ways, fully traditional, even classical, in its fidelity to the rabbinical tradition and its texts, and in this sense Yesha is the true realization of classical traditional Judaism. Put differently, no one, not even the most anti-Zionist detractor, can deny that Yesha is authentically based on Halachic traditions and codified authoritative texts.

This does not mean that all rabbinical authorities concur with Yesha theology or its political program, but even its opponents will not deny that messianic Zionism is based on traditional and legitimate rabbinical sources and texts. The understanding in rabbinical literature is that messianic times do not entail cosmic transformation. The authoritative sage Maimonides explained that the world will continue in its ordinary course in the messianic age, with the great difference that in messianic times "kingdom will return to Israel."[9] This has come to mean in rabbinical literature that the Jewish return from exile to the Land of Israel and Jewish sovereignty is, by itself, a messianic development. In the rabbinical view, messianic times and events are neither outside of empirical reality nor beyond normal rational understanding. One of the great and distinguished precursors of modern Zionism, Rabbi Zvi Hirsch Kalischer, a renowned Talmudist, explained,

> The redemption of Israel is not to be imagined as a sudden miracle, for which we long. The Almighty, blessed be His name, will not suddenly descend from on high and command His people to go forth. He will not send the Messiahs from heaven in a twinkling of an eye, to sound the great trumpet for the scattered of Israel to gather in Jerusalem . . . for the redemption of Israel will come by slow degrees and the ray of deliverance will shine forth gradually. [10]

Jewish messianism has an enormous this-worldly quality; the messianic era is a time of increased peace, prosperity, tranquility, and the restoration of Jewish sovereignty. Rabbinical and biblical narratives do talk about nations "beating their swords into plowshares" and the "resurrection of the dead," but these scenarios refer to *olam habah*, to the world to come, which is, in rabbinical understanding, a total cosmic transformation of the universe beyond human comprehension after the messianic era.

ACTIVE YESHA MESSIANISM

The originality and novelty of the Yesha movement has been its ability to wed traditional Jewish messianic belief with a radical program of militant settlement willing to challenge their Palestinian neighbors and international superpowers. Until the advent of the Yesha settler movement, religious Zionism was open to territorial compromise and eschewed militant activity. Religious Zionism was a passive partner to the Israeli establishment, content to have control over state religious institutions while leaving military and political decisions to the secular leadership. Yesha has transformed religious Zionism, which now seeks to fashion a state of Israel based on its vision of an unapologetic religious nationalism. Yesha militancy challenges both traditional Jewish passive and apocalyptic waiting for messianic redemption as well as secular Israeli realpolitik seeking compromise to foster improved Israeli standing in international relations and global business. Yesha messianic Zionism has another agenda, the rejection of practical political considerations to be replaced by militant faith and action on behalf of the mes-

sianic vision. Infused by faith and buttressed by widespread Israeli suspicion of Palestinian motives and the constant reality of terrorism,
Yesha Zionism has been able to maintain and strengthen its settlement
policy and attract supporters from all over the globe.

As the settlement enterprise continues, and with Yesha's increasing
support among nationalist parties, messianic Zionism has succeeded in
transforming religious Zionism. With few exceptions, religious Zionism
has adopted the theological and political views of Yesha theologians and
politicians. The old middle-of-the-road religious Zionists associated
with the Mizrachi party of the 1950s–1970s, with its willingness to affirm the messianic significance of the state of Israel but delay the implementation of that vision, no longer exist as a political entity. Religious
Zionists overwhelmingly vote for right-wing parties that support settlement activity and oppose territorial compromise. Supporters of Yesha in
the governing Likud party, together with more right-wing members of
the Jewish Home Party, form a strong nationalist bloc often opposing
the more moderate stance of Prime Minister Benjamin Netanyahu.[11]
Public support and political advocacy on behalf of the settler communities is now fully given by religious Zionists whether they live in the
West Bank, in pre-1948 Israel, or for that matter in the United States or
Europe.[12] Religious Zionists are no longer the quiescent minority they
once were, but are willing to aggressively confront the Israeli government in support of their religious nationalist agenda.

An example of this new confrontational style occurred during the
2005 disengagement from Gaza, when religious Zionists came en masse
to protest and physically confront police and military personnel. Avraham Shapiro, a former chief rabbi, issued a rabbinical edict stating that
it was against Jewish law for any soldier to cooperate with the military
authorities in evicting the Gaza settlers from their homes.[13] The rift
between religious Zionist Israelis and others was so serious that the
military and police recruited to execute the forcible removal of Gaza
settlers were generally secular Israelis, among them immigrants from
the former Soviet Union who did not identify with the settler religiosity
and attachment to the biblical land.[14] Visitors to the settlements and to
holy sites and shrines in Judea and Samaria are overwhelmingly religious Jews from all over Israel who identify and support the settlement
program. This is not to say that all religious Zionists are necessarily in
full support of Yesha policies. Nonetheless, the basic view of the state as

a religious entity, a harbinger of messianic evolution, and Jewish rights to settlement and sovereignty over the biblical land of Israel has become normative in religious Zionism. There are religious Zionist thinkers and rabbis who are in political disagreement with Yesha political tactics, style, and timing, but all follow the same religious liturgy and rituals, which extol the state as "the beginnings of messianic redemption."[15] The one religious Zionist party that opposed Yesha messianism, Meimad, led by the world-renowned Talmudist rabbis Yehudah Amital and Aron Lichtenstein, did not garner any significant support from the religious community and disappeared after a short existence.[16]

Apart from the religious community, Yesha settlement policies, if not tactics and religious talk, have attracted broad support in the Israeli mainline. No less a personage than Reuven Rivlin, the sitting president of Israel in 2014, supports settlements and in an interview with an American journalist explained, "It can't be 'occupied territory' if the land is your own."[17] In the final analysis, Yesha theology and culture have had an enormous impact on Jewish identity and self-understanding. Yesha has made it respectable for Jews to assert their rights over their ancestral homeland and reject the image of a wandering and homeless people. This transformation has not been easy for many Jews, and challenging as well for other religions and peoples who want to hold on to the image of the Jews as outsiders, a pariah people who need the intervention of outside powers. Yesha rejects this historical position and asserts that the Jewish people have entered the community of nations and, unlike in the recent and historical past, will vigorously, aggressively, and militarily defend themselves and assert their national rights to what they consider their ancestral homeland.

The Yesha policy of religious nationalism has led to a series of refinements, modifications, and leniencies in the traditional Halachic system of religious law. Judaism for almost two millennia of diaspora life was a religion of a pariah people, a religious minority without power or the responsibility of running a nation-state. Jewish religious law was essentially limited to the private sphere of family and synagogue and did not have to contend with the demands of a modern country. The Yesha movement rejects the Galut mentality of religion as a matter of private piety and seeks to create a modern, technologically functioning society, including providing electricity on the Sabbath, police, an army, transportation, and so on, which means that some of the traditional Sabbath and ritual demands have to be relaxed, at least for those who have to carry out these functions. Ethical rules and a legal system regarding war, corruption, robbery, and personal welfare for all citizens have to be established—issues not affecting a pariah and homeless people.[18] These goals and activities, uniting religion and personal ethics and morality with the ethics of a modern nation-state, are deeply opposed by the insular Haredim, who remain enmeshed in a diaspora mentality and religiosity.

HAREDI DISSENTERS

Haredi Jews, unlike the majority of secular Israelis, share a traditional religious lifestyle and commitment to the normative Halachic system with religious Zionists, and it is this group that is most fervently opposed theologically to Yesha messianic Zionism. For Haredi Jews, Zionism, secular or religious, is a revolt against Jewish destiny. Haredi Jews believe that no Jewish state, military preparedness, or international guarantee can protect the world's Jews from danger and persecution. The terrible error of religious Zionists is their refusal to acknowledge the abnormality and divine nature of Jewish suffering, which cannot be avoided. The dangerous illusion and sinfulness of religious messianic Zionists is their belief that a sovereign Jewish state can bring messianic redemption. For Haredi Jews, human beings, even with the best of intentions, cannot change the inherent and precarious situation of Jews until the divine and miraculous advent of messianic transformation. For Haredi religiosity, the rise of an independent state of Israel, the ingathering of millions of Jews to the biblical homeland, and even the Israeli control of Jerusalem and its holy sites are theologically meaningless. As a leading Haredi spokesperson put it after the Six-Day War,

> As long as Mashiach [the Messiah] has not come, the Golus [diaspora statelessness] continues. There is not a single word of the Prophets which has lost its eternal message. There is not a single sentence of our Sages which requires a new interpretation. Tragically so, it still is, as it was for two thousand years, "namely for our sins we were exiled from our land." True messianic redemption is overdue a thousand times. But as the messianic redemption has not come the Golus

continues and Kosel Ma'aravi [the Western Wall] remains to be our wailing wall.[19]

Haredim see religious Zionism and its embrace of the state of Israel as a heretical deviation from traditional Jewish faith. Haredim maintain that the Jewish state is a danger to faith, leading Jews to rely on themselves, on the secular authorities, and on the Israeli Defense Force rather than on divine salvation. Consequently, Haredim will not pledge loyalty to the state nor serve in the Israeli Army or offer prayers on behalf of leaders and soldiers. While Haredim admire the religious observance of Yesha settlers, they do not cooperate with them politically, and Haredi parliamentarians vote against Yesha interests in exchange for government support of Haredi communities and institutions. At best, Haredim see the state of Israel as a haven for persecuted Jews, but for them country has no religious standing. Haredim and religious Zionists have a complex and ambivalent relationship. Both are pious communities with deep commitment to Jewish tradition and practice, and though they disagree strongly on issues of religion and state, each admires the other's commitment. Religious Zionists respect the absolute fidelity to religious law among Haredim, and Haredim appreciate the ability of religious Zionists to maintain strong religious practice despite their commitment to a secular, antireligious state. Some former messianic Zionists who have been disappointed with the state's refusal to expand settlements and Israeli sovereignty have moved closer to Haredi Judaism, seeing in their Haredi brothers a purer form of Judaism uncontaminated by secularism and political compromise. Some elements in the Haredi world have moved closer to the Yesha position and now see events in Israel as having some element of evolving messianism. No one can predict what will occur, but should the two communities come closer together—and there are signs of this in the younger generation— the Yesha movement will be substantially strengthened demographically and politically. An important element in the recent political rapprochement between these religious communities is the growth of Haredi towns in the West Bank, which has resulted in Haredi politicians supporting Yesha positions in the Knesset, not for ideological reasons, but to secure financial support for their communities in Judea and Samaria. Haredim have an unusually high birth rate—families average between seven and twelve children—and this has caused housing shortages within the 1948 armistice lines, and low-cost housing is more read-ily available across the Green Line in the West Bank. The growth of the Haredi population in the West Bank will make it difficult for any government to depend on Haredi parties to support settlement evacua-tion.

SECULAR DISSENTERS

For most Israeli Jews, there is a deep ambivalence about the settlers and settlement policy. Surveys show that the majority of Israelis do not want to go back to the pre-1967 armistice lines and many see military and strategic value in those settlements built close to the 1949 lines.[20] And while the bulk of Israelis, though not formally religious, want Israel to be a Jewish state, they see Yesha settlements, the settlers, and their fundamentalist ideology as an impediment to having Israel function as a truly democratic state.[21] Moreover, secular Israelis see the continuing growth of the settlements as endangering the Jewishness of the state of Israel, as the West Bank occupation puts over a million Palestinians under Israeli jurisdiction. Even those secular Israelis who, for cultural, historical, or security reasons, support Yesha fear that continued occu-pation is leading to Israel's international isolation, particularly amid threats of economic boycott by the European Union, a major trading partner. Ofer Shelah, a Knesset member from the center Yesh Atid party, gave voice to this growing concern: "The settlements are an ob-stacle to a peace agreement, and this obstacle is growing. Israel pro-gresses daily towards becoming like South Africa. It is on the verge of a boycott of products—first those manufactured in the settlements and then those produced elsewhere in Israel." The fact of the matter is that even within Israel, among the leftist secular intelligentsia there is a refusal to use products manufactured in West Bank settlements.[22]

Opponents of the settlement enterprise, including deeply commit-ted Zionists, argue that Zionism is above all about having a Jewish state that is culturally and demographically Jewish. For this reason, these opponents of Yesha have demanded the uprooting of the West Bank Jewish communities, seeing continued Israeli occupation as leading eventually to a binational state of Arabs and Jews. This would destroy the Zionist dream of a national home for the Jewish people. Critics like

Gadi Taub concur and see Yesha as destroying the Zionist dream of a liberal democratic Israel, as Yesha is determined to create a theocratic state under rabbinical authority.[23] Gershom Gorenberg, a leading Israeli journalist who has deep knowledge of the settlement movement, argues in his book *The Unmaking of Israel* that the settlers are a dangerous trend in Jewish life, seeking to replace humanistic Zionism with a militant, mystic, and racist creed.[24] Taub and Gorenberg and many others like them in the Israeli academic and political elite, for all their criticism, are Zionists deeply committed to a Jewish homeland. Their criticism is Zionist, a different view of what ought to be the nature of a Jewish democratic state. In their support of a Jewish Zionist state, they are at one with settlers—both desire a Zionist state committed to Jewish identify and culture. For all their arguments, editorials, and criticism, this is ultimately a family dispute.

There are, however, Israelis—still a minority but active in academic and artistic circles—who maintain that it is Zionism itself that is the root of Israeli–Palestinian conflict and the settlements are but a symptom of the underlying racism inherent in an exclusively Jewish state. Ilan Pappé, a former professor at the University of Haifa and now at the University of Exeter in England, has argued that the basic Israeli national ideology of Zionism, which demands Jewish rights in the Land of Israel for Jews only, denying the essential rights of Palestinians, makes resolution of the conflict between Palestinians and Israelis impossible. In his view, as long as Zionist national ideology continues to be the justification for a Jewish state, the same settlement policies will continue. For Pappé, the settlements are just a logical continuation of Zionist ideology, which leads to territorial expansionism. In this view, both the settlements and Zionism are one issue. The Jewish state of Israel must dissolve and be replaced by a state not defined by religion, race, or ethnicity.[25] Benjamin Beit-Hallahmi, a professor of psychology at the University of Haifa, has argued that Zionism, begun as a humanistic movement to protect a persecuted, stateless minority, has become a colonial force oppressing the Palestinian people and must give way to a state not based upon religion or ethnicity.[26] For these anti-Zionists, the very idea of a Jewish state based upon a religious heritage is the underlying factor in the continuing conflict, and the settlements are a pernicious outgrowth of Zionist ideology.

ALLIES AND SUPPORTERS

The bulk of Yesha supporters are found among Modern Orthodox Jews in Israel and around the globe. Modern Orthodox Jews, both in Israel and abroad, increasingly identify with Yesha ideology and politics. Support of Yesha settlements has become a defining element in Modern Orthodox commitment. With few exceptions, to be a modern observing Orthodox Jew anywhere in the world means adhering to and agreeing with Yesha territorial rights and faith. Messianic Zionists are also not without international political and economic support. Mainline American Jewish organizations provide support for the settlement movement. Some of these groups dissent from certain positions the settlers take but provide funds and political support for the movement. Regular lobbying trips with thousands of participants travel to American congressional representatives to advocate for support of the settlements. American Jewish organizations such as the Hebron Fund, the One Israel Fund, and the Bet El Foundation raise millions of dollars to help the settlements, funding the construction of new schools, homes, and community centers all over the West Bank. There are a variety of smaller groups buying properties, sometimes clandestinely, in Arab East Jerusalem and in West Bank areas where the Palestinian Authority has prohibited sales to Israeli investors. American groups are also active in providing funds for the political campaigns of Yesha-backed candidates. A number of American Orthodox synagogues have instituted partnerships with settlement communities, providing aid and building playgrounds and schools. The Eretz Israel movement, an American lobbyist group, organizes tours highlighting the religious significance of the settlements in Judea and Samaria, which help maintain the religious loyalty and financial support of American Jews. Additionally, virtually all American Modern Orthodox high school graduates spend a gap year in Israeli religious Zionist schools and seminaries before going on to their university studies. As a result, not only is financial support provided, but a significant number of American Orthodox yeshiva graduates have settled in Yesha communities, among them several current leaders of the movement.

A surprising and important source of both political and financial support for the settlements has been American evangelical groups as well as Christian groups in Europe and Latin America. These groups have a complex relationship with the Jewish state. These Christian groups believe that the second coming of Jesus Christ can only occur when all the people of Israel are gathered once again in their ancestral land, and then the much-awaited end of time and wars and redemption promised in the Gospels will occur. These evangelical groups see it as their religious duty to aid the state of Israel in securing sovereignty over the full Land of Israel. In the end times, however, only those confessing faith in Jesus Christ as the Messiah will be saved from the terrors and wars and destruction that, according to their reading of Christian scripture, will occur in the final eschatological transformation. Be that as it may, these Christian groups have contributed millions of dollars and send hundreds of thousands of Christian religious tourists to Israel each year. With tens of millions of adherents, they are perhaps the most important reason for the strong American support of Israel and continued tolerance of settlement expansion. These groups, among them the politically well-connected Christians United for Israel, meet regularly with congressional leaders and representatives to argue on behalf of the settler communities and their political importance to American international interests. Reverend John Hagee, the founder and leader of Christians United for Israel, is also an important theological voice for Christian support of Israel. The group Christians for Israel International has officers and supporters in Europe, Asia, and Latin America and provides international political support but also sponsors trips and settlement activities. The organization Christian Friends of Israel Communities Heartland brings thousands of Christian pilgrims to Israel each year as part of the Sukkot Tabernacle festival. Their support for the settlements is clear and outright. The Christian Friends of Israel Communities website directly urges Christians "to connect with Jewish communities (settlements) in the heartland of Biblical Israel" and explains that "Judea and Samaria (the 'West Bank') is not occupied territory. It is the birthplace of the Jewish people."[27] By all accounts, evangelical Christians remain the strongest non-Jewish international supporters of Israel. Evangelical Christian support is rooted in the theological doctrine of many evangelical denominations and remains a source of profound comfort to the settlers, who generally feel besieged by the international community.

In conclusion, despite the opposition of Haredi religious Jews—and this opposition is weakening in the younger generation of Israeli-born children—and secular liberal Zionists who support the emergence of an independent Palestinian state, the essential Yesha political and religious agenda has become the accepted religious and political viewpoint of religious Jews all over the globe. Affirming traditional Halacha and culture, anchored in rabbinical texts and led by traditionalist rabbis, Yesha has transformed Judaisim and Jewishness. For world Jewry, it is no longer a fanatical sect, but normative religious Judaism.

TOWARD THE FUTURE: SETTLEMENTS AND THE ISRAELI–PALESTINIAN CONFLICT

In 1905, Negib Azoury, an Arab writer living in France, published a book in which he forecast a painful future for the Middle East.

> Two important phenomena, of the same nature but opposed, which have still not drawn anyone's attention, are emerging at this moment in Asiatic Turkey. They are the awakening of the Arab nation and the latent effort of the Jews to reconstitute on a very large scale the ancient kingdom of Israel. Both these movements are destined to fight each other continually until one of them wins. The fate of the entire world will depend on the final result of this struggle between these two peoples representing two contrary principles. [28]

Azoury was prescient in his analysis, and this conflict, going on for well over a century, is still unresolved. As the twenty-first century progresses, there is a strong European and American determination to broker a resolution. Both sides will have to compromise in any realistic agreement. The state of Israel will not be sovereign over the whole Land of Israel, and the Palestinians will have to renounce control over some of their sacred areas and will not be able to return to some of their ancestral homes. Any possible agreement to change boundaries for the establishment of an independent Palestinian state will be a severe disappointment to the messianic goals of religious Zionism.

There has been a series of internationally brokered agreements in the last fifty years—some expected to be spectacular breakthroughs, as with the famous 1993 Oslo Accords—but all ended in failure and increased tension, violence, and war. The international community, however, has not given up. There are currently, as in the past, numerous scenarios being presented that claim to be the solution to ending the conflict and having the parties agree to a peace settlement. Essentially, these many and often competing plans can be reduced to six major peace initiatives.

1. A Peace Agreement Based on the Pre-1967 Armistice Lines

Such an arrangement is supported particularly by nationalist Palestinian groups, along with some European governments and left-leaning European supporters of Palestinian statehood. The basis for this agreement is the Palestinian determination to deny Israel sovereignty over any area that, in the Palestinian view, was illegally captured, occupied, or annexed by Israel during the Six-Day War. This agreement demands that all parties return to the status quo at the time of the outbreak of hostilities and would mean that Israel would return all of Judea and Samaria to Palestinian control and cede sovereignty over East Jerusalem, with some provision for sharing authority over religious sites. In return, a full peace agreement between the two sides would take place.

This arrangement has been discussed, in some manner, for over fifty years with no success. Israelis, including both the religious population and the bulk of the secular population, would not consent to this arrangement, as Jerusalem and its Jewish places are considered essential to the Jewish state. No Israeli government could agree with this arrangement and stay in power. This type of peace proposal, demanding the removal of all settlements built after 1967, including those built with the purpose of encircling Jerusalem with Jewish enclaves, and the removal of hundreds of thousands of people from their homes in Judea and Samaria, would result in massive civil disobedience and civil war. Moreover, generals in the Israel Defense Force (IDF) would certainly veto this arrangement as it makes a surprise attack almost impossible to defend against, given the narrow borders of the pre-1967 lines. Although this type of agreement is still advocated by important Palestinian Authority officials and European diplomats, it has no chance of acceptance by the Israeli public and will not be implemented. This type of peace talk is actually welcomed and then ignored by the Yesha leadership, as it poses no realistic possibility of implementation and is no threat to settlement building and continued Israeli control of the West Bank.

2. Palestinian Autonomy and Union with the Kingdom of Jordan

This is the popular settlement view of how to end the conflict and broker a peace agreement. In this arrangement, all settlements would stay in place and Israel would maintain control and sovereignty over all of the West Bank, with Palestinian civil control over Palestinian towns and cities. Palestinians would be subjects of the Kingdom of Jordan—as was the case prior to 1967—have voting rights for the Jordanian parliament, and be governed by Jordanian law. This was one of the first Israeli plans put forward to resolve the conflict, but it was never accepted by either the Palestinians or the Jordanians, who were under pressure from Arab governments desiring Palestinian statehood and from the Jordanian elite, who saw the inclusion of Palestinians as a threat to local authority. Despite the full rejection of this plan by the Palestinians and all Arab governments, this remains an articulated Yesha plan.

3. Settlement Blocs and Territorial Exchange

This plan is very much on the international agenda and is strongly pushed by the United States. The goal is to establish a two-state solution whereby the large Israeli settlements would remain part of Israel in exchange for land in northern Israel that would be given to the newly formed independent Palestinian state. According to reports, land swaps would result in about 75–80 percent of the Jewish settler population remaining under Israeli sovereignty, with Jewish settlements in outlying areas uprooted and handed over to the new Palestinian state.[29] Another version of these arrangements, now absolutely rejected by the Palestinians, is that all Jewish settlers, even those in the areas to be given over to the new Palestinian state, would be able to remain in their homes and settlements, living as citizens or permanent residents in the new Palestinian state. This is the general outline of the plan, but serious issues remain, including the status of Jerusalem and its holy places, the status of Jewish holy places in the newly independent Palestinian state, and Israel's insistence that the Israeli military remains on the ground in the new Palestinian state.

Still, the Israeli government has indicated that though it has concerns about the details of territorial exchange, it is open to the plan.

Moderate elements in the Palestinian leadership as well voice interest and openness, but they have their concerns, particularly about the status of Jerusalem—which this plan, like others, avoids—and the right of Palestinian residents of pre-1948 territory to return to their ancestral homes. It appears that the moderate leadership in both the Israeli and Palestinian camps wants to pursue this plan, and if successful it would result in an independent Palestinian state and would leave most settlers in place. While moderates on both sides express interest, there are in both communities serious ideological objections. Nabil Abu Rudeineh, a leading spokesman for the Palestinian Authority representing the hard-line Palestinian position, called all settlements "illegal" and reiterated the right of the Palestinians to reclaim all the territory lost in the 1967 war.[30] Dani Dayan, the former head of the Yesha Council, objected to the plan, arguing that up to 150,000 Israelis would be forcibly removed from their homes, "which is morally repugnant and unacceptable to all."[31] Still, this plan, with all its unresolved issues, is a serious possibility, as it results in an independent Palestinian state with increased land in the Palestinian areas. For Israeli moderates and the business community, this arrangement would be welcome as it might remove the growing international economic boycott of Israeli products. For Israel, this agreement would mark a major breakthrough in which it would be forced to cede what it considers ancestral land and destroy a string of settlements on land given to the newly formed Palestinian state. Understandably, the plan is anathema to the messianic Zionist movement and would likely result in massive protests, civil disobedience, and possible violence between settlers and supporters of the agreement.

4. Annexation

All of the above arrangements have been discussed, attempted, and even provisionally agreed to by both parties, only to be rejected and discarded. Consequently, and despite all the peace talks and international pressure not to do so, annexation of the West Bank territories remains on the Israeli political agenda. The most well-known act of annexation was the Israeli incorporation of Arab East Jerusalem and its holy sites immediately after the cessation of the Six-Day War, resulting in one political authority for the combined city. All residents of the formerly Arab Jordanian Jerusalem became citizens of Israel, and all of Jerusalem is now under Israeli law and civil authority. While there is considerable opposition to West Bank annexation among the secular Israeli public, there is strong sentiment that towns and settlements in the environs of Jerusalem, like Efrat and Gush Etzion, should be incorporated and politically annexed to the Jewish state, some seeing this as a security matter while others see these territories as at the heart of Jewish history and identity.

The ideological settler movement supports annexation of all of the West Bank territories as the next and necessary step in the unfolding of the messianic process. But support for the annexation of Judea and Samaria is not limited to the Yesha messianic hard-liners. Beginning as a small nationalist right-wing political party in 2008, the Jewish Home Party, *Habayit Hayeyudi*, is now among the three or four largest parties in the Knesset and opposes an independent Palestinian state and supports annexing large portions of the West Bank. Their leader, Naftali Bennett, a forty-one-year-old software entrepreneur who was once a close associate of Prime Minister Netanyahu, proclaimed, "I will do everything in my power to make sure they [the Palestinians] never get a state."[32] His platform was clear: the two-state plan is dead and any talk of two states is a Palestinian delusion. Here was a duly elected official now articulating the Yesha position in the Knesset. These statements by Bennett illustrate how once-radical Yesha positions have come into the political mainstream. Bennett is not afraid of the international response to annexation, claiming that over time the international community will accept Israeli sovereignty in the West Bank. Bennett does not live in a settlement community, and while he wears the Orthodox kipah, he talks economics and politics and not messianic theology—he himself lives in Raanana, an upscale town in Israel's center—and many of his supporters live in urban centers far from the settlements. He has great support among religious Zionists, but he has managed to attract voters who do not share the settler religious ideology. The distrust and suspicion of Palestinian intentions are great among many middle-of-the-road Israelis, and the Jewish Home Party's platform, stressing the defensive and military advantage of holding on to the settlements, helped the party garner support from those not committed to the settler ideology.

Talk of annexation is not limited to the Jewish Home Party but also several Knesset members of the governing Likud party. One of the most outspoken leaders in the annexation movement is Tzipi Hotovely, a member of the governing Likud party and the current deputy minister of transportation. Hotovely, who is a prominent younger minister, shares Bennett's opposition to an independent Palestinian state, and she too insists that Israel must annex large parts of the territories. I interviewed Minister Hotovely in December 2013 and asked her how Israel will fare if, as seems likely, a severe economic boycott of Israeli goods and the imposition of international sanctions would occur in the event of annexation. Minister Hotovely did not deny the possibility of a boycott but maintained that the current West Bank situation of military occupation and lack of full civil rights for the Palestinian residents is a greater threat to Israel's international standing than annexation. Hotovely told me that the occupation in the West Bank with its dual system of law, one for Israeli settlers and another for local Palestinian Arabs, is viewed by the international community as an Israeli version of apartheid. She acknowledged that the current setup of military governance is immoral and is impossible to maintain. Annexation, she argued, would result in civil rights for all residents and would remove the danger of international censure. When I pointed out that the incorporation of over a million Palestinian Arabs now living in the West Bank as full citizens in an Israeli state would compromise her view of a Jewish state, Hotovely told me that this a short-term issue and that millions of Jews from all over the world will be making Aliyah and will correct any demographic imbalance. This mass migration does not seem to be occurring, but here one sees the influence of messianic faith in political decisions. Hotovely and the supporters of annexation are faithful Zionists who believe that, come what may, their religious vision will be realized.[33] The annexation option has received significant legal support from the official Israeli "Report on the Legal Status of Building in Judea and Samaria," popularly referred to as the Levy Report, on the legality of Israeli authority in the West Bank. The report, based upon the findings of a three-member commission headed by Supreme Court Justice Edmond Levy, concluded that Israel has full legal rights to establish settlements in the West Bank according to international law and that the area in Judea and Samaria is not an "occupied territory."[34] The Israeli judiciary has strong global standing and is truly independent of the political leadership, and this has given the annexation proponents serious standing.

Still, the annexation option is disregarded in the Western media, in international diplomacy, and among secular Israelis themselves. Israeli business and academic elites see annexation as a dangerous religious fantasy that will never come about. As they say, "Who wants another two million Arabs in the Jewish state?" Moreover, an international economic and cultural boycott would certainly ensue and have disastrous effects on the Israeli economy. Still, if no acceptable peace agreement can be brokered and if Israel continues to see a Palestinian state of any kind as a stronghold for Hamas extremists, as is now the case in Hamas-controlled Gaza, annexation may well be seen as the best Israeli option. In the Israeli view, annexation would mean legally incorporating the West Bank areas where the bulk of the settlements are located into the Israeli state and giving Israeli citizenship to Palestinians Arabs living in these areas. Areas with large Palestinian populations would not be annexed but would be guaranteed local political autonomy under Israeli rule but no rights as citizens.

5. The Status Quo Option

With other options not available, the preferred Yesha position is to continue the situation as is, albeit with increased autonomy for Palestinians in their towns, cities, and villages but continuing de facto Israeli sovereignty over the entire West Bank. Dani Dayan, a mainline Yesha leader not known for his messianic views, insisted in the *New York Times* that the Israeli settlements are an irreversible fact and that given the political realities on both sides a final status agreement is not a realistic possibility at this time. Rather than lamenting the current situation, Dayan argued, both sides should acknowledge the reality and work together to ensure security and greater economic and employment opportunities for the Palestinians. Dayan put it this way: "While the status quo is not anyone's ideal, it is immeasurably better than any other feasible alternative."[35]

In important ways, this Yesha view is shared—though never acknowledged—by both Israeli political center and many Palestinian politicians. No one really likes the current situation, but neither does anyone foresee a more advantageous arrangement. The Israeli have the territory and what they see as superior security, and the Arab parties, deeply patient, see things eventually leading to an Arab majority and a one-state arrangement. Any agreement at this time would mean both parties surrendering critical ideological and territorial positions, resulting in internal civil conflict for both. Consequently, there is little real movement for a full-scale peace agreement. Both side articulate well-worn peace sentiments but end up never compromising on the critical issues of borders, the Palestinian right of return, and the acceptance of Israel as an exclusively Jewish state. One veteran Israeli diplomat I interviewed explained that all the past agreements failed not because they were faulty but because all the parties involved were content with the current situation. The future is always hard to predict. In the Middle East, it is impossible to have a true sense of the future. Will America and the international community impose a settlement, or will the current imbroglio continue?

The 2014 Gaza War between Israel and the Hamas militants controlling Gaza made an agreement on territorial change and an independent Palestinian state even more problematic. After having relinquished control of Gaza to the Palestinians in 2005, Israel found itself at war when Hamas fired thousands of rockets all over Israel, causing panic in the population. This was the first time since Israel was established that population centers like Tel Aviv were under fire. Israel responded with a massive bombardment of Hamas sites in which almost two thousand people were killed, including many civilians and children. Despite the condemnation of the international community, Israel continued the bombing until a cease-fire was agreed upon. Despite the loss of life and the international outcry, the Israeli government's war policy was supported by an overwhelming majority. Even some of the leading Israeli advocates for peace, reconciliation, and a Palestinian state supported the government's war policy.[36]

The Hamas attacks on Israel from Gaza, an area Israel freely and unilaterally left to Palestinian control, resulted in many otherwise sympathetic Israeli peace advocates questioning whether giving up the territory controlled after the 1967 Six-Day War would result in a cessation of violence and real peace. The Gaza pullout, once heralded by secular settlement opponents as a prelude to Palestinian statehood, was mocked by Michael Freund in an editorial: "Despite countless warnings at the time that the Gaza pullout would bring disaster, Sharon pressed ahead, demolishing more than 20 flourishing Jewish communities and withdrawing the IDF from the Strip. This foolhardy move paved the way for the Hamas takeover of Gaza in 2007, a turning point that has had calamitous consequences for Israel ever since." Freund went on to argue that the Gaza War doomed the two-state arrangement. Israelis now know, he wrote, that "uprooting Jews from their homes and turning over territory to the Palestinians only serves to pour fuel on the fire burning in the hearts of our enemies."[37] Freund is a fervent settlement supporter, but his words make sense in the Israeli context and resonate with Israelis who do not share his politics.

MESSIANISM, ZIONISM, AND THE FUTURE OF THE JEWISH STATE OF ISRAEL

What are the future prospects for the Yesha movement? If the status quo continues or the annexation option is enacted, the Yesha enterprise will grow and expand. In the absence of any possible agreement with the Palestinians, the Israeli government will see no advantage in limiting settlement expansion, and this will only encourage Yesha messianic aspirations and serve to confirm their religious faith. Still, this scenario is hard to imagine given the enormous diplomatic and economic pressure on the Israeli government and Israeli business interests. There is a strong movement in the European Union to refuse imports from Israel, and there is an American movement to divest from Israeli companies, particularly refusing to fund new high-tech startups. For this reason, Israeli business leaders have been especially supportive of peace initiatives and have made the argument that a viable Israeli economy requires territorial and ideological compromise. Although Prime Minister Netanyahu has publicly referred to the boycott and divestment initiative as the new anti-Semitism, government officials—and even some Yesha leaders—acknowledge its danger. But the status quo continues, and an Israeli policy of limited annexation is not unimaginable. As long as the Palestinians refuse to acknowledge Israel as a Jewish state with sovereignty over Jewish sacred places, no peace arrangement can be had and religious nationalists will likely not be forced to abandon their positions or evacuate settlements. Their messianic dreams will continue.

In the Israeli political center, there is significant will to seek accommodation with the Palestinian Authority, to end the violent conflict, and restore Israel's international moral and economic standing. If a referendum were held to cede territory or eliminate outlying settlements, it would likely carry a majority. However, there is another internal issue that does not make the headlines: the changed officer composition of the Israeli Army. Estimates are that religious Zionists now constitute about 40 percent of the elite officer corps and that the Israel Defense Force as a whole is now increasingly composed of religious recruits. In 2010, the Israeli Army publication *Bamahane* reported that 12.5 percent of all company commanders were residents of settlements, and some of the most fervent supporters of messianic Zionism are on the highest rungs of the military leadership.[38] Should a peace agreement require the military to remove settlers, it is extremely unlikely that these officers would go along with civilian orders, nor would many of the religious soldiers in the lower ranks. Both the military and the government know this. The refusal of many religious soldiers to go along with the Gaza evacuations has had a large effect on military and political thinking. If anything, the opposition to a pullout has grown, and the military itself is now less able and less willing to go along with a political decision to evacuate. The removal of nine thousand residents from Gaza would be nothing compared to the forced removal of well over a hundred thousand residents from outlying settlements like Hebron, Bet El, and Ofra. Like most Western armies, the IDF no longer attracts as many talented and well-educated secular recruits as it did in the past. But for religious Zionist young people, serving in the army, joining elite units, and defending the sacred land is a religious duty, and their overriding loyalty is to their rabbis and religious edicts, not to secular military authority.

Still, it is the Middle East, and one never knows. Should an agreement involving territorial exchanges and Palestinian statehood be reached, it would severely challenge Yesha communities and their vision of a messianic future. How might the faithful react to what they would see as a treasonous and unholy destruction of their settlements, religious faith, and messianic dreams? How could believers make sense of, be reconciled to, and live with the dissolution of their communities, personal aspirations, and religious goals? How would believers react to the betrayal of a state that, for them, has such sacred and transformative power? Disappointment and loss are always difficult, but they are particularly painful in the case of religious visions. With scores of settlements throughout the West Bank holding a current population of close to five hundred thousand people, including third- and fourth-generation children, and with hundreds of thousands of religious Zionists all over the state of Israel, any forced removal of West Bank residents would result in a major crisis for the state. The educational, religious, and social institutions of religious Zionist society are all so deeply dependent on their messianic theology that the evacuation of settlements, declaring them illegal and not part of the state of Israel, would challenge the continuity of messianic Zionism as a viable religious and political movement.

There are three possible Yesha responses to the loss of this religious vision: (1) theological and political surrender, (2) theological reinterpretation and political realignment, and (3) militant rebellion and transformation.

THEOLOGICAL AND POLITICAL SURRENDER

Theological surrender means that, in the event of the downfall of the movement, former believers acknowledge that their faith was misplaced and their political program has no future. They were wrong, misled, and their belief in the state of Israel as the harbinger of messianic redemption was not to be realized. Theological surrender is not pleasant because it means confirming that one has been living in illusion and dedicated oneself to a false messianic program. Still, as Festinger and his associates have shown, surrender is a way out of living with disappointment and cognitive dissonance.[39] Some elements of theological surrender were seen after the Gaza disengagement and continue whenever the Israeli government dismantles "illegal" settlements or destroys unapproved expansion. Some particularly pious Yesha followers have moved to a Haredi understanding of Jewish theology, claiming that the state of Israel is a secular entity and can never have a central place in the unfolding of messianic transformation. This move will continue should agreements demanding territorial compromise take place, and some Yesha followers will sever their religious connection with the Zionist state and take up an older passive apocalyptic view of messianic redemption. Others will renounce religious nationalism and return to an older, more mainstream political Zionism.

THEOLOGICAL REINTERPRETATION

Theological reinterpretation is a complex phenomenon and has elements of surrender and resignation while still maintaining belief in the movement. In response to the loss of settlements, settlers and followers acknowledge that their policies have been rejected and will not be immediately implemented. However, unlike with theological surrender, there is neither rejection of their faith nor abandonment of their goals. Rather, there are elaborate theological and sociological reinterpretations to make sense of the current setback. In this possible response, Yesha activists would go along with government policy, still holding on to their messianic faith and aspirations. Only now, the messianic end time would be redefined and reinterpreted. Disappointed believers might say, "Our program and faith are pure and will be realized, but we moved too fast, too aggressively." In this fashion, Yesha ideology remains realistic and redefines defeat as but a delay of eventual vindication. Reinterpretation, too, is ongoing. Rabbi Yoel Bin-Nun,[40] a former leader of the messianic Gush Emmunim group, has renounced violence ideology and now supports territorial compromise. Bin-Nun, still a religious nationalist, now argues that the way to messianic redemption involves compromise, nonviolence, and even momentary defeat. For Bin-Nun, it is certain that in time messianic transformation will take place and the biblical Land of Israel will be restored to the Jewish people. For now, the faithful need patience, love for their fellows, and greater piety. Others, such as Rabbi Yehuda Amital of the Mount Etzion Yeshiva, put this in more mystical terms, explaining that in time religious faith, piety, and sacrifice will surely move heaven to bring messianic transformation.[41] In the meantime, both of these rabbis urge compromise and nonviolence. Many settlers will likely go along with theological reinterpretation, as it provides both optimism for the future and explanation for disappointment.

MILITANT TRANSFORMATION

Radical settlers will not accept surrender, compromise, or reinterpretation of their doctrine, faith, and politics. Radical believers see compromise and reinterpretation as a weak-willed abandonment of authentic faith, and they view those who surrender Yesha belief as heretics and cowards. Radicals see militant action, including protests and violent responses, as legitimate tactics to realize their political and religious goals. Their goal is to transform society to their beliefs. Consequently, violent confrontations between militant settlers and government forces are likely if territory and sovereignty are ceded to a new Palestinian state. As I explained earlier, there is much in biblical and Talmudic theology to support Yesha radicalism and violence, and militants expand on these doctrines to justify violent resistance. The potential for violence is now increased by the existence of hundreds of young radicals, who were brought up in the settlements and see them as their home. For these people, the West Bank occupation is normal, everyday life, and they do not view themselves as living in an "illegal occupied area." And unlike their parents, they are less concerned with religious and political restraints on violence but see violent confrontation as a legitimate and necessary response to maintain their homes and institutions and ideological commitments.[42]

The Talmud teaches that only fools predict the future, and indeed no pundit or scholar, no matter how imaginative, can tell us how politics and statecraft will turn out. History records many happenings thought impossible that became reality. Many events predicted by scholars and statesmen turn out to be illusions. In our contemporary times as well, those labeled terrorists at one point, such as Nelson Mandela in South Africa, Ho Chi Minh in Vietnam, and Menachem Begin in Israel, turn out to be national and international heroes to be emulated. And much-heralded initiatives like the Iraq War, the Oslo Accords, and the diplomatic and covert operations to thwart international terrorism against civilians have ended in failure. The American civil rights movement, the gay rights movement, and the historic Zionist movement for a Jewish state, all once thought to be worthy but unattainable efforts, have become established political and social reality. Transformative movements, whether political, social, or religious, similarly share this unpredictable history. Some commentators see messianic Zionism as a passing phrase, an exuberant messianism fueled by Holocaust memories and military victories, soon to be tempered by political reality; others see this triumphant Zionism as a dangerous misreading of Jewish religion; and still others view the Yesha movement as an unethical, even immoral, movement that jeopardizes the future of the state of Israel. All these positions are well argued and seem to have merit, but only the future will decide.

A NOTE ON RESEARCH METHODS

The methodology for this study was conducted in the Weberian tradition of humanistic social science using the perspective of the sociology of knowledge.[1] The goal is to present an interpretive understanding—what Max Weber referred to as *verstehende Soziologie*—of the motives, meanings, theology, and lifestyle of the West Bank Yesha settlers. The book presents the world of the settlers as they see it and gives an insider's view of settlers' faith, politics, and commitment to radical religious Zionism. The objective was to discover the underlying assumptions of the religious and political worldview that motivates settler culture, faith, and commitment.[2] To research and develop an interpretive understanding of the Yesha world and to the present the settlers' "construction of reality,"[3] participant observation and interviews were conducted in a variety of settlement communities, from radical and militant communities populated by disciples of Meir Kahane and Yitzchak Ginsburg to several moderate middle-class settlements such as Kedumim in Samaria. The research was conducted over a period of three years, and I resided in ten different settlements, some for a period of a few weeks and others for extended weekends. I participated in communal activities and prayer meetings and was often a guest at Sabbath dinners, which allowed for extended conversations. I visited sacred sites with the settlers and even once participated in a demonstration against the government to experience political action as a seeming settler. Everyone in the settlements I visited knew I was researching a book, but because I am religiously knowledgeable, know Hebrew, and am familiar with Orthodox culture, I was welcomed and people were willing to be interviewed. I occasionally challenged the assumptions of settlers, but they trusted I would accurately report their worldview.

I conducted over fifty formal interviews with both ordinary settlers and settler rabbis and political leaders. I spoke to several nationalist prosettlement members of the Israeli parliament, only one of whom was willing to be quoted. These interviews sometimes were just conversations that illustrated that the settlement movement now had political standing. The interviews with Yesha leaders and residents consisted of both focused and open-ended questions. I asked about motivations for moving to the settlements, about the dangerous conditions of life in the isolated communities, and about the settlers' views on Palestinian rights to the disputed land. The interviews were not recorded in order not to limit the responses. Instead, I kept copious and exact notes, both during and after interviews, to have an accurate record. Some of the interviews are explicitly discussed in chapter 4. In addition to the formal interviews, I had dozens of everyday conversations with people in the synagogues, in the supermarkets, and on the bus to and from settlements. These informal interactions gave me fuller insight into the settler world and prepared me for the sometimes more scripted interviews with settler leaders and rabbis.

Much reporting on the settler movement ignores their deep religiosity and traditionalism. Yesha is indeed a radical political movement but one based on traditional and normative Talmudic and rabbinical theology. The settlers' adherence to the rabbinical tradition gives them, in their view, great legitimacy and a measure of acceptance in all sectors of Orthodox Judaism. In this book, I examined these important theological texts and consider how Yesha's militant theology and political program is based on their creative reading and reinterpretation of the traditional Jewish theological canon. Consequently, the book discusses both the writings of the forerunners of religious Zionism and the work of contemporary Yesha theologians and ideologues, who have fashioned an innovative but still radical Zionism. A deep grounding in classical and contemporary Jewish theological thinking is critical to unveiling the sources of the settler worldview. Consequently, this work covers sociological themes while also presenting the classical and contemporary rabbinical writings that form the theological basis for Israeli settlements.

This is a book about the settlers living in Judea and Samaria, but it is also about the continuing Middle East conflict, which has global significance. In the concluding chapter, I looked at the views of Israeli politicians and diplomats and the significance of worldwide Jewish and evangelical Christian political and monetary support of the settlement enterprise. My goal is to foster better understanding of religious nationalism and to help make sense of the Middle East conflict. The book offers no fixed answers, nor does it make political judgments. The objective is to provide much-needed information for informed and reflective political understanding and decision making.

NOTES

INTRODUCTION

1. *Yesha* is a Hebrew acronym for Judea, Samaria, and Gaza, areas in which Jewish settlements were established in formerly Palestinian areas after the 1967 war.

2. Max Weber, *Ancient Judaism*, trans. and ed. Hans Gerth and Don Martindale (Glencoe, IL: Free Press, 1952).

3. See Kalman Neuman, "Which Way for Religious Zionism?," in *Religious Zionism Post Disengagement: Future Directions*, ed. Chaim Waxman, 133–55 (New York: Yeshiva University Press, 2008).

4. For a defense and justification of settler violence, see Era Rapaport, *Letter from Tel Mond Prison: An Israeli Settler Defends His Act of Terror*, ed. William B. Helmreich (New York: Free Press, 1996).

5. One longtime Israeli critic, the editor-in-chief of the prestigious *Haaretz* newpaper, when asked why he so strongly objected to the settlers' politics and religiosity, put it this way: "Of the state being run according to a crazy-state policy that doesn't rely on strategic, political, economic, demographic or geographic considerations. These factors taken together form the 'game of nations' that has been in existence since creation. Settler leaders in their destructive naïveté believe that the State of Israel can afford to play the game by other rules. . . . This is I think where the zealots of the Bar-Kochba revolt [a failed Jewish rebellion in Judea in 132–136 that resulted in the removal of Jews from the Holy Land] went wrong and—this is the settlers' mistake." David Landau, *Haaretz*, February 27, 2015, 10. An example of the growing international pressure is the the decision of the European Union to require products from the

Israeli settlements to be so labeled so that they can be boycotted and refused to be sold in European states. See https://euobserver.com/foreign/128367.

6. Max Weber, "Science as a Vocation," in *Max Weber*, ed. Hans Gerth and C. Wright Mills (New York: Oxford University Press, 1958).

1. THE RISE OF THE SETTLEMENTS

1. The Hebrew Bible records this promise that traditional Jews consider binding to this day: "I will ratify my covenant between me and you and between your offspring after you, throughout their generations as an everlasting covenant to be a God to you and your offspring after you and I will give you and your offspring after you the land of your sojourns—the whole of the Land of Canaan—as an everlasting possession and I will be a God to them" (Gen. 17:7–8, *Tanach: Stone Edition*, ed. Noson Scherman [Brooklyn, NY: Mesorah, 2007]).

2. Throughout the centuries, there was some Jewish migration to the Holy Land. These Jewish émigrés were usually particularly religious types who wanted to live in the sacred environs of the Holy Land. These migrations sometimes consisted of dozens of families or a group of followers of a particular rabbi, but these groups had no plan for Jewish independence or political authority.

3. For a history of Zionism and the emergence of the state of Israel, see Amos Perlmutter, *Israel: The Partitioned State* (New York: Charles Scribner, 1985), chap. 2.

4. Charles Selengut, *Sacred Fury: Understanding Religious Violence* (Lanham, MD: Rowman & Littlefield, 2008), 26–29.

5. Ismail R. al-Faruqi, "Islam and Zionism," in *Voices of Resurgent Islam*, ed. John S. Esposito (New York: Oxford University Press, 1983), 261–67.

6. Shlomo Chaim HaCohen Aviner, comp., *Torat Eretz Yisrael: The Teachings of Harav Tzvi Yehuda Hacohen Kook*, with commentary by David Samson, trans. Tzvi Fishman (Jerusalem: Torat Eretz Yisrael, 1991), 137.

7. Tom Segev, *1967: Israel, the War, and the Year That Transformed the Middle East* (New York: Henry Holt, 2007).

8. For the complete response to the victory and its aftermath, see Gershom Gorenberg, *The Accidental Empire: Israel and the Birth of the Settlements, 1967–1977* (New York: Henry Holt, 2006).

9. Shimon Schwab, *Selected Writings* (Lakewood, NJ: CIS Publications, 1988), 115. Unlike Schwab, Modern Orthodox rabbis were sympathetic to religious Zionism but still counseled restraint and messianic waiting.

10. Aviner, *Torat Eretz Yisrael*, chap. 8.

11. For discussion of this pivotal event, see Gabi Taub, *The Settlers and the Struggle over the Meaning of Zionism* (New Haven, CT: Yale University Press, 2010), 41–44.

12. This prayer in Hebrew, known as the "Prayer for the State of Israel," is recited in all Orthodox Zionist synagogues in Israel and in all Modern Orthodox communities all over the world. See *The Koren Siddur* (Jerusalem: Koren, 2009), 522.

13. Samuel C. Heilman and Menachem Friedman, "Religious Fundamentalism and Religious Jews: The Case of the Haredim," in *Fundamentalisms Observed*, ed. Martin E. Marty and R. Scott Appleby, 197–264 (Chicago: University of Chicago Press, 1991).

14. Precise population data is difficult to verify, but scholars and diplomats operate with those of the Foundation for Middle East Peace. See "Israeli Settlements: Settlements Population in the West Bank," Jewish Virtual Library, http://www.jewishvirtuallibrary.org/jsource/Peace/wbsettle.html. See also Dani Dayan, "Israel's Settlers Are Here to Stay," *New York Times*, July 26, 2012, where the demography of the settlements is considered.

15. For a presentation of this position, see Benjamin Beit-Hallahmi, *Original Sins: Reflections on the History of Zionism and Israel* (Brooklyn, NY: Olive Branch Press, 1993), chap. 9.

16. This was a sentiment I found among the severest critics of the movement: a respect for their commitment to historical memory and a high regard for the settlers' willingness to sacrifice personal advantage for what they perceived as the national welfare. This attitude often went along with complete rejection of their theologically based politics.

17. For an excellent narrative of these events, see Gorenberg, *Accidental Empire*, chap. 4.

18. See Mark Langfan, "What Are We Thinking," Israel National News, December 26, 2013, http://www.israelnationalnews.com/News/News.aspx/175506#.VOyURrPF_OU.

19. Gorenberg, *Accidental Empire*, chap. 4.

20. For a discussion of the earlier cooperation of moderate and left-leaning Israelis with the development of the settlements, see Idith Zertal and Akiva Eldor, *Lords of the Land: The War over Israel's Settlements in the Occupied Territories* (New York: Nation Books, 2007).

21. See Gorenberg, *Accidental Empire*, chap. 4. Gorenberg has nicely illustrated the "euphoria" among Israel's military and political elite immediately following the Six-Day War.

22. Zertal and Eldor, *Lords of the Land*, chap. 1.

23. Jerold Auerbach, *Hebron Jews: Memory and Conflict in the Land of Israel* (Lanham, MD: Rowman & Littlefield, 2007).

24. Zertal and Eldor, *Lords of the Land*, chap. 4.

25. Emanuel Sivan, *Radical Islam: Medieval Theology and Modern Politics* (New Haven, CT: Yale University Press, 1985).

26. "Hebron: History & Overview," Jewish Virtual Library, http://www. jewishvirtuallibrary.org/jsource/History/hebron.html.

27. See the Ofra community website at http://www.ofra.org.il/english and "Ofra," Wikipedia, http://en.wikipedia.org/wiki/Ofra.

28. Zertal and Eldor, *Lords of the Land*, 47.

29. Taub, *The Settlers*, 37–64.

30. Dayan, "Israel's Settlers Are Here to Stay." See also "Israeli Settlements: Settlements Population in the West Bank," Jewish Virtual Library, http://www.jewishvirtuallibrary.org/jsource/Peace/wbsettle.html.

2. FROM ZIONISM TO MESSIANIC NATIONALISM

1. Michael Wyschogrod, *The Body of Faith: God and the People Israel* (Lanham, MD: Rowman & Littlefield, 2000).

2. Nosson Scherman and Meir Zlotowitz, *The Complete Machzor Yom Kippur* (Brooklyn, NY: Mesorah, 1993), 178.

3. Peter Schafer, *The Mystery of Bar Kokba* (Tübingen: Morh, 2003).

4. Jody Meyers, *Seeking Zion: Modernity and Messianic Activism in the Writing of Tsevi Hirsch Kalischer* (Oxford: Littman Library of Jewish Civilization, 2003), 8.

5. Arthur Hertzberg, ed., *The Zionist Idea: A Historical Analysis and Reader* (New York: Atheneum, 1971).

6. Charles Selengut, "By Torah Alone: Yeshivah Fundamentalism in Jewish Life," in *Accounting for Fundamentalism: The Dynamic Character of a Movement*, ed. Martin E. Marty and R. Scott Appleby, 236–63 (Chicago: University of Chicago Press, 1994).

7. Hertzberg, *Zionist Idea*, 215–16.

8. Hertzberg in *The Zionist Idea* argues, correctly, that secular Zionism, while avowedly nonreligious, was greatly influenced by biblical messianism.

9. Elchonon Wasserman, *Yalkut Mamorim V'Mictavim* (Brooklyn, n.d.), 121.

10. Selengut, "By Torah Alone," 245.

11. See Hertzberg, *Zionist Idea*, 416–34, for the early Mizrachi Zionist theological and political worldview.

12. For the significance of these radical activists in establishing the settlement movement, see Gorenberg, *Accidental Empire*, chap. 3.

13. See Aviner, *Torat Eretz Yisrael*, for a full statement and elaboration of settler religious Zionism. See also Yossi Klein Halevi, *Like Dreamers: The Story of the Israeli Paratroopers Who Reunited Jerusalem and Divided a Nation* (New York: HarperCollins, 2013), 114–26, for a report on the emergence of the culture of messianic Zionism.

14. Gideon Aram, "Jewish Zionist Fundamentalism: The Bloc of the Faithful in Israel (Gush Emunim)," in *Fundamentalisms Observed*, ed. Martin Marty and R. Scott Appleby, 265–344 (Chicago: University of Chicago Press, 1991).

15. This view is elaborated in Aviner, *Torat Eretz Yisrael*, 155–200. See the excellent review of relevant biblical, Talmudic, and contemporary literature in Ya'akov Moshe Bergman, *A Question of Redemption: Can the Modern State of Israel Be the Beginning of Redemption* (Jerusalem: Kol Mevaser, 2000), esp. 121–40.

16. The changes came in increased ritual observance and stronger modesty taboos and in the enforced segregation of genders. For an insightful view, see Halevi, *Like Dreamers*, 19–23.

17. Bergman, *Question of Redemption*, 123.

18. Bergman, *Question of Redemption*, 124.

19. Waldenberg, quoted in Bergman, *Question of Redemption*, 128.

20. Aviner, *Torat Eretz Yisrael*, 278.

21. For religious Zionists, the economic and technological successes of Israel are distinct signs of divine blessing. See Dan Senor and Saul Singer, *Start-Up Nation: The Story of Israel's Economic Miracle* (New York: Twelve, 2011).

22. Rabbinical commentators quote Mark Twain, who wrote, about his 1867 visit to the Holy Land, "Palestine is desolate and unlovely. And why should it be otherwise? Can the curse of the deity beautify a land?" in his travel book *The Innocents Abroad*. This is, according to the rabbinical commentators, the natural condition of the biblical land when the Jewish people were exiled. The return of the Jews resulted in the transformation of the land and the economy. See Bergman, *A Question of Redemption*, 126–27.

23. Aviner, *Torat Eretz Yisrael*, 155–77.

24. Aviner, *Torat Eretz Yisrael*, 286–87.

25. An extended discussion of this perspective is elaborated in Aaron Soloveitchik, "Yishuv Eretz Yisrael v'Milchemet Mitzvah B'Zman Hazeh," *Ohr Hamizrach* 49 (October 2003): 9–19.

26. Soloveitchik, "Yishuv Eretz Yisrael," 13.

27. Quoted in Aviner, *Torah Eretz Yisrael*, 185.

28. See Chaim Levinson and Nir Hasson, "Rightists Launch 'Day of Rage' over West Bank Outpost Demolition," Haaretz.com, March 3, 2011, http://

www.haaretz.com/news/national/rightists-launch-day-of-rage-over-west-bank-outpost-demolition-1.346849.

29. See Zalman Melamed, *Yesh Shoalim* (Bet El, Israel: Kiryat Hayeshiva, 1998). Melamed is a highly respected and widely read rabbinical leader of messianic Zionism, a renowned Talmudist, and perhaps the leading advocate of the political and psychological changes needed in Jewish society as the messianic process unfolds. In his essays, Melamed utilizes biblical and rabbinical texts to justify the Yesha political worldview.

30. This is a complicated issue with lots of public objection and behind-the-scenes understanding and approval. See Max Blumenthal, "46% of Jewish Israelis Support Settler "Price Tag" Terror, Congress Blames Palestinians for Incitement," March 22, 2011, http://maxblumenthal.com/2011/03/48-of-jewish-israelis-support-settler-price-tag-terror-congress-blames-palestinians-for-incitement/, for a discussion of this issue. See also "Poll: 46% in Favor of "Price Tag," Ynetnews.com, March 28, 2011, http://www.ynetnews.com/articles/0,7340,L-4048459,00.html. The poll explains, "While most seculars oppose 'price tag' activities (36% in favor, 57% against), most traditional, national-religious and ultra-Orthodox Jews believe these actions are justified (55%, 70% and 71%, respectively)."

31. Rabbi Eliezer Melamed, "Islam Lives by the Sword," reprinted at http://icevikings.blogspot.ca/2009/09/islam-lives-by-sword-by-rabbi-eliezer.html. See also "The Truth on Israel Palestinian Conflict," https://www.youtube.com/watch?v=Nc8EjQEpZ3s.

32. Melamed, "Islam Lives by the Sword."

33. Ibid.

34. Eliezer Don-Yehiya, "The Book and the Sword: The Nationalist Yeshivot and Political Radicalism in Israel," in *Accounting for Fundamentalism: The Dynamic Character of Movements*, ed. Martin E. Marty and R. Scott Appleby, 264–302 (Chicago: University of Chicago Press, 1994).

35. Zalman Melamed, "The Limits of Democracy," in Melamed, *Yesh Shoalim*, 29.

36. Chaim Levinson, "Dismantle Israeli Democracy and Replace It with Jewish Law, Says Settler Leader," *Haaretz*, January 8, 2012, http://www.haaretz.com/print-edition/news/dismantle-israeli-democracy-and-replace-it-with-jewish-law-says-settler-leader-1.406035. One formerly prominent Yesha rabbi, Yoel Bin-Nun, was forced from any position or standing in the movement because he argued for a synthesis of democracy and religion and advocated for a measure of Palestinian rights. One settler said, "He is no longer one of us." Indeed, there are settlements where he is no longer welcome.

37. For an informed and insightful treatment of the Gaza disengagement and its aftermath, see Taub, *Settlers and the Struggle over the Meaning of Zionism*, 119–52.

38. For an extended discussion of the theological issues regarding the disengagement, see Avraham Shapiro and Aharon Lichtenstein, "A Rabbinic Exchange on the Gaza Disengagement," *Tradition* 40, no. 1 (2007): 17–44.

3. FAITH, CULTURE, AND COMMUNITY LIFE

1. *Tanach: Stone Edition*, ed. Noson Scherman (Brooklyn, NY: Mesorah, 2007).

2. Peter L. Berger, "Some Sociological Comments on Theological Education," *Perspective* 9, no. 2 (Summer 1968): 127–38.

3. See the Ariel Center for Policy Research at http://www.acpr.org.il/ for a secular position supporting settlements.

4. For a description and analysis of these programs, see Gorenberg, *Unmaking of Israel*.

5. "University Professor Sparks Ire with His Comparison to Hitler Youth," JTA, April 30, 1995, http://www.jta.org/1995/04/30/archive/university-professor-sparks-ire-with-his-comparison-to-hitler-youth.

6. See Judy Maltz, "Boycott = Anti-Semitism? Some Israelis Avoid Settlemnt Products Too," Haaretz.com, February 24, 2014, http://www.haaretz.com/news/features/.premium-1.575929.

7. The theological and political justifications for the settlement worldview are powerfully expressed by Zalman Melamed in his collected essays, *Yesh Shoalim* (Bet El, Israel: Yeshivat, 1997).

8. Melamed, *Yesh Shoalim*, 29–30.

9. Rav Shlomo Aviner, *Am V'Artzo* (Bet El, Israel: Sifriat Chavah, 2010), 69–83; see also 217–19.

10. For an intellectual biography unpacking Kook's Kabbalistic Zionism, see Yehudah Mirsky, *Rav Kook: Mystic in an Age of Revolution* (New Haven, CT: Yale University Press, 2014).

11. Yehudah Mirsky, "Messianic Temptations," *Jewish Ideas Daily*, April 7, 2011, http://www.jewishideasdaily.com/859/features/messianic-temptations/.

12. For an insightful biography of Amital, see Elyashev Reichner, *By Faith Alone: The Story of Rabbi Yehuda Amital* (Jerusalem: Koren, 2011). See also the important exchange on theology and politics in Shapiro and Lichtenstein, "Rabbinic Exchange on the Gaza Disengagement," 17–44. Amital, now deceased, and Lichtenstein were the heads of the Gush Etzion Yeshiva, located in one of the first areas to be settled outside of the 1949 armistice lines. Gush

Etzion is a religious Zionist seminary, but over time both of these rabbi leaders have distanced themselves from earlier activist messianism, though they have maintained allegiance to the religious and messianic potentialities of the state of Israel.

13. For a critical Yesha view of the Jewish diaspora, see Aviner, *Am V'Artzo*, 9–66.

14. See data and discussion on Jewish–Gentile intermarriage and the lack of Jewish identification in "A Portrait of Jewish Americans," Pew Forum, October 1, 2013, http://www.pewforum.org/2013/10/01/jewish-american-beliefs-attitudes-culture-survey/.

15. Aviner, *Am V'Artzo*, esp. 9–50.

16. Rappaport, *Letters from Tel Mond Prison*, 24.

17. For an example of dialogue and reconciliation by a settler rabbi, see the life of Rabbi Menachem Froman, who was one of the founders of Gush Em-munim (http://jerusalempeacemakers2008.jerusalempeacemakers.org/froman/home.html). The community of Efrat, which has a large number of American Jewish émigrés, has also established cooperative relations with local Arab communities. Some of the exchanges between important Palestinian and settler personalities have taken place out of the public eye. See a report on one such meeting in Klein Halevy, *Like Dreamers*, 496–500.

18. Aviner, *Torat Eretz Yisrael*, 197, emphasis in original.

19. Ephraim Urbach, "Jewish Doctrines and Practices in Halachic and Aqadic Literature," in *Violence and Death in the Jewish Experience: Papers Prepared for a Seminar on Violence and Defense in Jewish History and Contemporary Life*, ed. Salo W. Baton and George S. Wise (Philadelphia: Jewish Publication Society, 1977). See also Selengut, *Sacred Fury*, chap. 1, for an analysis of the concept of "holy war" in religious theology.

20. Selengut, *Sacred Fury*, 25–30.

21. Al-Faruqi, "Islam and Zionism," 261–67.

22. Charles Selengut and Yigal Carmon, "Judaism, Islam and the Middle East Conflict," in *Jewish-Muslim Encounters: History, Philosophy and Culture*, ed. Charles Selengut, 102–18 (St. Paul, MN: Paragon, 2001).

23. Yair Altman, "Itamar Massacre: Fogel Family Butchered while Sleeping," Ynetnews.com, March 13, 2011, http://www.ynetnews.com/articles/0,7340,L-4041237,00.html.

24. See "Palestinian Political Violence," Wikipedia http://en.wikipedia.org/wiki/Palestinian_political_violence.

25. For the role of martyrdom in Jewish theological thinking, see Selengut, *Sacred Fury*, 201–4.

26. Tal Bashan, "Larger Than Life," *Jerusalem Post*, July 25, 2013, http://www.jpost.com/In-Jerusalem/Features/Larger-than-life-321001.

27. See Nachman Ben Yehudah, *The Masada Myth: Collective Memory and Mythmaking in Israel* (Madison: University of Wisconsin Press, 1995).

28. For a contemporary theological defense of this position, see Soloveitchik, "Yishuv Eretz Yisrael." See also Yecheskel Levenstein, *Ohr Yecheskel*, vol. 3 (B'nai Brak, Israel: Ponavitch Yeshiva, 1977).

29. For an overview and discussion of this worldview, see Yitzchak Blau, "Ploughshares into Swords: Contemporary Religious Zionists and Moral Constraints," *Tradition* 34, no. 4 (2000): 39–60.

30. Aviner, *Torat Eretz Yisrael*, 175.

31. David Weisburd, *Jewish Settler Violence: Deviance as Social Reaction* (University Park: Pennsylvania State University Press, 1989). See also Anti-Defamation League, "Price Tag Attacks," December 22, 2014, http://www.adl.org/israel-international/israel-middle-east/content/backgroundersarticles/price-tag-attacks.html#.VO4--7PF9Cw.

32. Aviner, *Torat Eretz Yisrael*, 168.

33. Aviner, *Torat Eretz Yisrael*, 168.

34. Klein Halevy, *Like Dreamers*, 307.

4. INSIDE THE SETTLEMENTS: PORTRAITS, CONVERSATIONS, AND EXPERIENCES

1. Yifa Yaakov, "Radical Settlers Discuss Legitimacy of Killing Soldiers," *Times of Israel*, May 7, 2014, http://www.timesofisrael.com/radical-settlers-discuss-legitimacy-of-killing-soldiers/.

2. The intelligence officer was referring to Taub, *Settlers*, which views the settlers as an antidemocratic movement seeking to destroy the state's democratic institutions. Taub also plays down the messianic aspirations of the movement and does not view the settler movement as an authentic religious group.

3. Israeli scholars estimate that fewer than 50 percent of all Israelis have ever visited a settlement in Judea and Samaria. Most secular Israeli civilians have no personal acquaintances or family in the West Bank settlements.

4. This position is taken most prominently by Rabbi Yehuda Amital of the Mount Etzion Yeshiva. See Reichner, *By Faith Alone*, 197–210. Interestingly, Rabbi Shlomo Aviner, known as a fervent settler, also takes a gradualist view of Temple building and encourages muting messianic rhetoric. See Aviner, *Am V'Artzo*.

5. This does not mean that all settlers agree with the full messianic program. Still, residents in Judea and Samaria appear to be fully committed to settlement building and expansion and Jewish sovereignty in the Land of Is-

rael. Theologically moderate settlers also view the state as having messianic dimensions.

6. For an interesting history, see Auerbach, *Hebron Jews*.

7. Known as the Hebron Fund, this organization raises money to support Hebron and its residents from all over the globe. See, for example, their publication, *Hebron Today*, https://hebronfund.org/.

8. See Caroline Glick, "Ignoring Failure in Gaza," August 8, 2008, http://carolineglick.com/ignoring_failure_in_gaza/.

9. See "Shalhevet Pass Remembered," Hebron Fund, March 13, 2013, https://www.hebronfund.org/blog/41-shalhevet-pass-remembered.

10. Rabbi Ari Weiss is a pseudonym I have given to the rabbi. All public figures have been identified in this book, but individuals who are not in the public realm have been given pseudonyms.

11. See Havat Gil'ad website at http://havatgilad.rjews.net/.

12. For more on the Oslo Accords, see the PBS *Frontline* page on the negotiations: http://www.pbs.org/wgbh/pages/frontline/shows/oslo/negotiations/.

13. For a case study detailing this phenomenon, see Palestinian Media Watch, "Demonization of Jews/Israelis," http://www.palwatch.org/main.aspx?fi=762.

14. Dani Dayan, "A Settler Leader, Worldly and Pragmatic," *New York Times*, August 17, 2012, http://www.nytimes.com/2012/08/18/world/middleeast/dani-dayan-worldly-and-pragmatic-leader-of-israels-settler-movement.html.

15. Meir Kahane, *Listen World, Listen Jew* (Jerusalem: Institute of the Jewish Idea, 1978), 21.

16. "Kahane," *Authentic Jewish Idea*, January–February 1988, 22.

17. This shrine was subsequently removed by the Israeli government. For a news report of the removal activities, see Joel Greenberg, "Israel Destroys Shrine to Mosque Gunman," *New York Times*, December 30, 1999, http://www.nytimes.com/1999/12/30/world/israel-destroys-shrine-to-mosque-gunman.html.

18. For a discussion of these events and Amir's justification, see Michael Karpin and Ina Friedman, *Murder in the Name of God: The Plot to Kill Yitzhak Rabin* (New York: Henry Holt, 1998), esp. 102–13.

19. Yitzchak Ginsburg, "Boruch Hagever," in *Baruch Hagever*, ed. Michael Ben Horin, 19–47 (Jerusalem: Medinat Yehudah, 1995).

20. Many of the young radicals knew little about the cabalistic underpinnings of Ginsburg's theology of violence but saw him as a charismatic rabbi whose ideas and directions were to be followed. Ginsburg was able to pick up

elements in Hasidic and cabalistic theology that could be interpreted to justify a "momentary violation of religious law and morality for a higher good."

21. "Amos Oz: Hilltop Youth Are Neo-Nazis," *Jerusalem Post*, May 10, 2014, http://www.jpost.com/National-News/Amos-Oz-Hilltop-youth-are-Hebrew-neo-Nazis-351830.

22. Ibid.

23. For a discussion of Israeli responses and sentiments, see http://www.maxblummenthal.com/2011,03,48.

24. Giulio Meotti, "In 'Defense' of 'Price Tag' Action," Op-Ed, Why Israel?, http://www.whyisrael.org/2014/01/27/op-ed-in-defense-of-price-tag-actions.

25. See Tessa Satherley,"'The Simple Jew': The 'Price Tag' Phenomenon, Vigilantism, and Rabbi Yitzchak Ginsburgh's Political Kabbalah," *Melilah: Manchester Journal of Jewish Studies* 10 (2913): 57–91, for an informed discussion of the kabbalistic themes in Ginsburg's writings.

5. JUDAISM, RELIGIOUS NATIONALISM, AND THE MIDDLE EAST CONFLICT

1. Nosson Scherman and Meir Zlotowitz, *The Complete Artscroll Siddur* (Brooklyn, New York: Mesorah, 1985), 679.

2. Quoted in Aviner, *Torat Eretz Yisrael*, 164. See also 205–8 for an analysis of Maimonides' view of religious obligations to live and settle in the Land of Israel.

3. See Aviner, *Torat Eretz Yisrael*, chap. 8, where the rabbinical and Talmudic views are discussed and elaborated. See also Bergman, *A Question of Redemption*, 41–47, where these views are analyzed.

4. Aviner, *Torat Eretz Yisrael*, 175.

5. Aviner, *Torat Eretz Yisrael*, 156.

6. Bergman, *A Question of Redemption*, 138.

7. The messianic fervor was great in 1948. Members of the non-Zionists community, such as Agudath Israel representatives, also signed the Israeli Declaration of Independence. At that time, only extreme anti-Zionist, like the Neturei Karta group, denounced the state of Israel.

8. See particularly the statement by the famed rabbi and Talmudist Yakov Moshe Charlap in Aviner, *Torat Eretz Yisrael*, 180–81.

9. Maimonides, *Mishnah Torah*, "Hilchot Melachim," 12:1.

10. "Rabbi Samuel Mohilever," in Hertzberg, *Zionist Idea*, 398.

11. For a portrait of this new support for religious nationalism, see David Remnick, "The Party Faithful," *New Yorker*, January 21, 2013, 38–44.

12. See, for example, "North American Jews Show Great Enthusiasm toward Buying a Home in Yesha," Amana, http://www.amana.co.il/?CategoryID=106&ArticleID=369. Prayer and financial support are ongoing realities among religious Zionist communities all over the Jewish world.

13. Shapiro and Lichtenstein, "Rabbinic Exchange on the Gaza Disengagement."

14. See Ed O'Loughlin, "Insults Fly as Gaza Stand-off Continues," *Sydney Morning Herald*, August 17, 2005, http://www.smh.com.au/news/world/insults-fly-as-gaza-standoff-intensifies/2005/08/16/1123958065076.html. Interviews with former residents confirm this.

15. For an interesting case study, see Reichner, *By Faith Alone*. Rabbi Yehudah Amital broke with the Yesha leadership, but his theological positions are based on religious nationalism.

16. The party no longer exists, but a history of its emergence and disappearance can be found at the Jewish Virtual Library, http://www.jewishvirtual library.org/jsource/Politics/Meimad.html. Meimad was strongly supported by secular parties, who saw them as a religious alternative to Yesha activist religious nationalism.

17. David Remnick, "The One State Solution," *New Yorker*, November 17, 2014, 46.

18. For the interaction of modernity and Orthodox law, see the Zomet Institute, http://www.zomet.org.il.

19. Schwab, *Selected Writings*, 115.

20. See, for example, Ryan Jones, "Poll: Most Israelis Support Settlements," *Israel Today*, June 14, 2012, http://www.israeltoday.co.il/NewsItem/tabid/178/nid/23257/Default.aspx?article=related_stories.

21. In the Israeli context, most Jews who identify as secular will still perform selected rituals, observe religious holidays in some fashion, and identify with the Jewish religion.

22. Attila Somfalvi, "Yesh Atid MK Warns Occupation Will Turn Israel into S. Africa," Ynetnews.com, June 12, 2013, http://www.ynetnews.com/articles/0,7340,L-4391662,00.html. See also "West Bank—Israel Settlements Also Face Pressure from Within," *Vos Iz Neias?*, February 12, 2014, http://www.vosizneias.com/155078/2014/02/12/west-bank-israeli-settlements-also-face-pressure-from-within/. Interestingly, it is virtually impossible to buy products manufactured in West Bank settlements in any upscale Tel Aviv shop.

23. Taub, in *Settlers*, takes a particularly strong view, seeing the settlers as endangering the continuity of Israel as a democratic state.

24. Gorenberg, *Unmaking of Israel*.

25. International Solidarity Movement, "Second Interview with Ilan Pappé: 'The Basic Israel Ideology—Zionism—Is the Problem,'" July 11, 2013, http://

palsolidarity.org/2013/07/interview-with-ilan-pappe-the-basic-israeli-ideology-zionism-is-the-problem/.

26. Benjamin Beit-Hallahmi, *Original Sins: Reflections on the History of Zionism and Israel* (New York: Olive Branch Press, 1993).

27. See http://www.cfoic.com. This statement appears directly on the organization's website. See also the important organizations headed by John Hagee (http://www.jhm.org). Hagee is an important link between the American Congress and Israeli religious nationalism. One Israel Fund (http://www.one israelfund.org/) stresses its commitment to the settlements as the vanguard of the Jewish people and is a major American fundraiser for Yesha projects. In addition, each Orthodox religious Zionist community has its own fundraising and lobbying organization.

28. . Quoted in Arthur Hertzberg, *The Fate of Zionism: A Secular Future for Israel and Palestine* (San Francisco: HarperOne, 2003), 63–64.

29. "US Framework Deal Puts 75–80% of Settlers under Israeli Rule," *Times of Israel*, January 31, 2014, http://www.timesofisrael.com/us-framework-deal-puts-75-80-of-settlers-under-israeli-rule/.

30. Elad Benari, "Abbas Spokesman: Netanyahu Speech Offered Nothing New," *Israel National News*, March 5, 2014, http://www.israelnationalnews.com/News/News.aspx/178128#.VPB3krPF9Cw.

31. Lazar Berman, "Yesha Council: Indyk Misleading, Will Uproot 150,000," *Times of Israel*, January 31, 2014, http://www.timesofisrael.com/yesha-council-indyk-misleading-will-uproot-150000/.

32. Quoted in Remnick, "The Party Faithful," 38.

33. See Tova Dvorin, "MK Hotovely: Ya'alon Shouldn't Have Apologized to Kerry," *Israel National News*, January 15, 2014, http://www.israelnationalnews.com/News/News.aspx/176333#.VPB94rPF9Cw, for the worldview of a young right-wing politician and supporter of religious messianic nationalism.

34. The official English translation of the report can be found at http://fmep.org/resource/report-of-the-sharm-el-sheikh-fact-finding-committee/. See also Kenneth Levin, "The Levy Report: A Vital Beginning," *Jerusalem Post*, November 11, 2012, http://www.jpost.com/Opinion/Columnists/The-Levy-Report-A-vital-beginning.

35. Dayan, "Israel's Settlers Are Here to Stay."

36. Gorenberg, *Unmaking of Israel*, 144.

37. Michael Freund, "The Gush Katif War," Op-Ed, *Vos Iz Neias?*, August 4, 2014, http://www.vosizneias.com/174262/2014/08/04/jerusalem-oped-the-gush-katif-war/.

38. For a report and discussion on the changing culture of the Israeli armed forces, see Yuval Elbashan, "Between Commander and Commandment: Is the IDF Becoming More Religious?," *Haaretz*, May 3, 2013, http://www.haaretz.

com/weekend/week-s-end/between-commander-and-commandment-is-the-idf-becoming-more-religious.premium-1.519054.

39. Leon Festinger, Henry W. Rieken, and Stanley Schacter, *When Prophecy Fails* (Minneapolis: University of Minnesota Press, 1956).

40. Maayana Miskin, "Rabbi: 'Price Tag' Will Get Us All Expelled," *Israel National News*, January 16, 2014, http://www.israelnationalnews.com/News/News.aspx/176359#.VPCT5bPF9Cw. Bin-Nun explained that settler violence will lead to expulsions from Judea and Samaria. Militant settlers see Bin-Nun as a heretic and traitor to messianic Zionism.

41. Reichner, *By Faith Alone*, 197–210.

42. For an in-depth and academic analysis on the rise of settler violence in the younger generation, see Carl Yonker, "The Hilltop Youth: Policy Memo," March 12, 2012, http://www.academia.edu/4348742/THE_HILLTOP_YOUTH_Policy_Memorandum.

A NOTE ON RESEARCH METHODS

1. Weber, "Science as a Vocation."

2. Clifford Geertz, *The Interpretation of Cultures* (New York: Basic Books, 1973).

3. Peter L. Berger and Thomas Luckman, *The Social Construction of Reality* (New York: Doubleday, 1967).

GLOSSARY

Aliyah. Literally, "to go up," the term now refers to Jews leaving their home countries and places of birth and emigrating to the Land of Israel. Aliyah is a central Zionist goal and value.

Beit Hamikdash. The Jerusalem Temple, which served as the ancient Jewish cultural center and was located on the Temple Mount, which Judaism considers its most sacred religious site. The second and last-standing Temple was destroyed in 70 CE, and that day is still commemorated as a day of national mourning.

Charisma. A quality of leadership and personality that endows a religious or political leader with unquestioned authority. The pronouncements of charismatic leaders are considered true and divinely inspired by their followers. Charisma can be used for good or evil purposes.

Chiloni. A secular Jew living in the modern state of Israel who is religiously nonobservant.

Christian Zionists. Christians who believe that the establishment of the modern state of Israel and the return of Jews to the Holy Land is in accordance with scriptural doctrine and is a prelude to the second coming of Christ.

Cognitive Dissonance. The psychological stress experienced when an individual holds two opinions or beliefs—cognitions—that are contradictory and mutually exclusive; for example, being a pacifist who is opposed to war and also supporting a nation's war.

Dar al-Islam. The "abode of Islam," referring to territory under Muslim sovereignty where the rules of Islam are legally established.

Dati. A religious Orthodox Zionist Jew who lives in the mother state of Israel.

Eretz Yisrael. Literally, the "Land of Israel," referring to the territory of the modern state of Israel and the areas of Judea and Samaria in the West Bank, which religious Zionists consider the Promised Land bequeathed by God to the Jewish people.

Galut. The Jewish diaspora, referring to lands outside of Israel where Jews have settled and created communities.

Gush Emmunim. Literally, the "Bloc of the True Believers," Zionist nationalist settlers who have established Jewish communities in the Israeli-controlled West Bank, in the ancient Jewish areas of Judea and Samaria.

Halacha. The collected canon of Jewish religious law based on the Bible and the Talmud and followed by Orthodox Jews.

Haram al Sharif. The Muslim holy site in Jerusalem where, according to tradition, the Prophet Muhammad ascended to heaven.

Haredim. Ultra-Orthodox religious Jews who reject political and religious Zionism and believe that Jews must wait passively for a supernatural messianic world transformation.

Jihad. A Muslim religious obligation involving a "struggle" for faith and overcoming evil. Jihad can be a psychological or political struggle, but it can also involve war and violence on behalf of religion and faith.

Judea and Samaria. Biblical names for West Bank areas under Jordanian rule prior to the 1967 Six-Day War and now under Israeli control and claimed by the settlers as an integral part of the Jewish Zionist homeland.

Kach. A militant political party, now declared illegal by the Israeli government, founded by Rabbi Meir Kahane and committed to the transfer of Arabs to Muslim lands.

Kiddush Hashem. Literally, the "sanctification of God's name," a concept in Jewish theology of bringing honor to God by performing acts of charity and surrendering to God's will to the point of religious martyrdom.

Labor Party. The secular Zionist socialist party that governed Israel until 1977 and is opposed to the settlement movement and its religious Zionist agenda.

Masada. An ancient fortification located in the Judean desert where Jewish rebels committed mass suicide in 73 CE to avoid capture by an invading Roman army.

Messianic Zionism. A religious Zionist position that asserts Jewish settlement building and political sovereignty over the biblical Land of Israel will result in the coming of the messianic age described in Jewish scripture.

Milchemet Mitzvah. An obligatory war ordained by God in which killing and destruction are sanctioned by divine command.

Price Tag. Civil disobedience or violent protest actions taken by militant Israeli settlers as retribution for attacks on settlers or settlement property.

Religious Zionism. A sector of the Zionist movement that views the rise of the modern state of Israel in 1948 as a divine event and the beginning of messianic redemption.

Temple Mount. The traditional site of the ancient Jewish Temple in Jerusalem.

Yesha. Hebrew acronym for Judea, Samaria, and Gaza, lands occupied by Israel after the 1967 Six-Day War and the name used by the settler movement.

Yeshiva. A religious seminary of higher Jewish learning where the traditional texts of the Bible and Talmud are studied.

Zionism. The religious and political movement that supports the establishment of the state of Israel as the national home for Jews.

KEY FIGURES

Amir, Yigal. A former law student and militant Zionist who in 1995 assassinated the then prime minister of Israel, Yitzhak Rabin, over Rabin's willingness to exchange land for a peace agreement with the Palestinian Authority. Amit is now serving a life sentence in an Israeli prison.

Amital, Yehuda, and Aron Lichtenstein. Distinguished rabbis and leaders of the Gush Etzion Yeshiva and moderate religious Zionist theologians who opposed militant messianic Zionism.

Begin, Menachem. Former nationalist prime minister of Israel from 1977 to 1983 who was a strong ideological supporter of West Bank settlements.

Bennett, Naftali. Head of the nationalist Jewish Home Party. Bennett is a young and influential political voice in Israel and a firm ideological and political supporter of settlements.

Bin-Nun, Yoel. Rabbi and former militant member of the Ofra settlement who broke with militant Zionism and seeks a peace accommodation with the Palestinians.

Ginsburg, Yitzchak. Rabbi and kabbalist who authored theological tracts justifying renegade religious violence in defense of Jewish settlements

Herzl, Theodor. The founder of modern political Zionism. Herzl organized the first Zionist congress in 1897 and was the visionary behind the movement for a Jewish homeland.

Hotovely, Tzipi. Member of the Israeli Knesset representing the nationalist faction of the Likud party. Hotovely is a strong supporter of settlements but also advocates Palestinian local autonomy.

Kahane, Meir. An American rabbi and militant Zionist who immigrated to Israel, where he founded the ultranationalist Kach party, which advocated expulsion of Arabs from Israel. Kahane was assassinated during a visit to New York City in 1990 by an al-Qaeda operative.

Kook, Abraham Isaac. Famed rabbi and kabbalist who served as chief rabbi of Palestine during the period of the British Mandate and authored many influential works on the spiritual connection between Jews and the Land of Israel.

Kook, Tzvi Yehuda. Son of Abraham Isaac Kook, head of the Merkaz Harav Yeshiva, and charismatic rabbi who is seen as the spiritual father of the settler movement. Kook's students went on to establish Gush Emmunim, and they continue to be leaders of militant Zionism.

Maimonides, Moses. Medieval Jewish philosopher, physician, and Talmudist who authored the compendium of Jewish religious law, *Mishnah Torah*, still studied and acknowledged as authoritative in contemporary Judaism.

Melamed, Zalman. Rabbi of the Bet El Community in Samaria and a leading advocate for Jewish settlement in Judea and Samaria.

Marzel, Boruch. Radical settler who lives in Hebron and advocates expatriation from Israel for Arabs. In the 2015 Israeli elections, he ran as a Knesset candidate with the nationalist religious Yachad party.

Peres, Shimon. Former Israeli president and prime minister of the leftist Labor party. Peres was politically opposed to the settlements but was sympathetic to the settlers' nationalist goals and at times aided them in establishing outposts in the West Bank.

Porat, Hanan. Rabbi and war hero who was instrumental in establishing the Gush Etzion settlement, which was the forerunner for the establishment of settlements all over the West Bank.

Rabin, Yitzhak. A former prime minister of Israel and opponent of settlements who was assassinated in 1995 by Yigal Amir, a militant settler advocate.

Shapiro, Avraham. Former chief rabbi of Israel and head of the nationalist Merkaz Harav Yeshiva. Shapiro was a highly respected Rabbi who encouraged religious soldiers to disobey orders to evacuate Jewish residents from Gaza in 2005.

Soloveitchik, Aron. Professor of Talmud at Yeshiva University and a renowned American Jewish theologian and rabbi who was a committed supporter of settlements and Yesha ideology.

INDEX

ABOUT THE AUTHOR

Charles Selengut is an expert on the sociology, psychology, and politics of religious fundamentalism and new religious movements and has published articles and monographs on the significance of Islamic and Jewish fundamentalism in international relations. His book *Sacred Fury: Understanding Religious Violence* explains the nature and motivation behind the current rise of religious conflict and faith-driven violence across the globe. He has been a member of the MacArthur Foundation–sponsored University of Chicago Project on Fundamentalism and has lectured at conferences and universities across Europe, Asia, and the United States. He has been active in interreligious studies and is the editor of *Jewish-Muslim Encounters: History, Philosophy, and Culture*, a volume based on an international conference held in Cordoba, Spain, that he organized with Professor Muntaz Ahmad. He is professor of sociology at the College of Morris in Randolph, New Jersey, is visiting professor at Drew University in Madison, New Jersey, and was a National Endowment for the Humanities Fellow at Harvard University.